The Best Plant-Based Ve
Burgers, Wings, Tacos, Gyr

VEGAN STREET EATS

Will Edmond
Vegan Chef & Travel Host

with Austyn Rich

PAGE STREET
PUBLISHING CO.

PAGE STREET
PUBLISHING CO.

Distributed by Macmillan, sales in Canada by The Canadian Manda Group.

28 27 26 25 24   1 2 3 4 5

ISBN-13: 978-164567-855-7

ISBN-10: 1-64567-855-5

Library of Congress Control Number: 2023936951

Edited by Franny Donington

Cover and book design by Emma Hardy for Page Street Publishing Co.

Photography by Toni Zernick. Lifestyle photography by David Singeorzan

Printed and bound in the United States of America

This book is dedicated to my parents, Willie and Shirley Edmond; my grand-mother, Bennie Mitchell; my great-grandmother, Margrett Washington; and my Aunt Lucile Peoples, for always being my inspiration. I love all of you.

To my partner, Austyn Rich, thank you for putting up with me. I know that sometimes I can be all over the place with my ideas, but you help reel them in and keep me focused. You are the best!

To my sister, Courtnee Edmond, and nephew, Christian Earl Edmond-Williams, thanks for being my biggest fans.

And to my online community, thank you for following all my recipe creations over the last few years.

CON-TENTS

Northern Treats   75

Foodie Globetrotting   89

Sweet Thangs   119

Keep It Saucy   143

Introduction

This cookbook is tailored for someone always on the go, eager to experience street food from around the world.

Choosing vegan street food as the heart of this cookbook stems from my global travels, a quest to bring you a taste of the amazing flavors I've experienced. I wanted this cookbook to be your culinary companion, simple yet bursting with flavor, ensuring your plant-based journey is a vibrant and ever-evolving feast.

Cooking has been one of my favorite activities since I was young. While I've never excelled at painting or drawing, I've found my artistry in creating dishes that nourish both the body and soul. Cooking unleashes my creative side and satisfies the geek in me, as it is rooted in science, especially baking. Experimenting with different spices and measurements is a joy, resulting in both amazing and okay outcomes—but that's the beauty of loving the kitchen.

I've always dreamt of having my own book and TV show, and now, as you read this book, one of those dreams is coming true. Initially hesitant to share my creations, I was encouraged by friends to share my recipes with the world, which brought unexpected blessings. Adding to the inspiration, I'm writing this cookbook from my great-grandparents' land, a place passed down for a century—a full-circle moment. The love for cooking, imparted by my family, has now reached a broader audience.

I want to thank my online community, my family, friends and especially my partner, Austyn Rich, who has been a tremendous help in coauthoring this cookbook with me.

To my cherished community and supporters, your belief in me and your decision to bring this cookbook into your home mean the world. Thank you for being a part of this delicious adventure—I'm thrilled to share it with you.

SLAMMIN' SAMMICHES

Indulge in the world of delectable eats with these sammiches. Every bite is bursting with flavor and plant-based enchantment. Get ready to take your sammich game to new heights!

Ultimate Crispy Chick'n Biscuit

Serves 6

I remember Granny (Madea) waking up early around five a.m. to make homemade biscuits. She would wrap them up and we'd take them on the bus to eat while on our way to school. I also remember my great-grandma (Big Momma) cooking some of the best fried chicken. When Big Momma prepared her chicken, it was always crispy. You can find my vegan version on page 12; it was one of the most viral chicken-substitute recipes on the internet. Since I'm vegan, I took what I learned to make this delicious meal come together. Combining these flaky, soft biscuits with my viral crispy chicken makes for the most delicious, Southern-inspired sandwich. Catch the recipe on the next page to put it all together.

½ tsp fresh lemon juice

1 cup (240 ml) unflavored, unsweetened oat milk (or any plant-based milk of your choice)

2 cups (250 g) organic all-purpose, unenriched, unbleached flour, plus more for dusting

1 tbsp (14 g) baking powder

½ tsp baking soda

¾ tsp sea salt

¼ cup (57 g) vegan butter, very cold

Warm vegan butter, for brushing

Southern Crispy Fried Chick'n (page 12)

Preheat your oven to 450°F (230°C). Add the lemon juice to your cup of oat milk; this is how you'll make your vegan buttermilk.

In a large bowl, combine your flour, baking powder, baking soda and salt, and mix well. Add the cold butter to the flour mixture. Mix in the butter until it breaks down into small crumbs. Very cold butter is important to minimize melting while mixing.

Make a small indentation in the flour mixture. Add small amounts of the buttermilk mixture, mixing after each pour, until a pliable dough is formed. Your biscuit batter will be slightly sticky. You can rest your dough for 2 to 4 minutes on lightly floured waxed paper or any floured surface—do not overflour.

Knead the dough six to eight times. Cut or pull apart the dough and make 1-inch (2.5-cm)–thick disks. Don't handle them too much, or you'll lose the consistency. Place the biscuits on a baking sheet, forming two rows and ensuring the biscuits touch one another. Brush the tops with warm vegan butter. Be sure to make a small indention in the middle of each biscuit, so they'll all rise uniformly.

Bake on the lower rack of your oven for 15 to 17 minutes, or until your biscuits have risen and are golden brown. Serve with my Southern Crispy Fried Chick'n, your favorite vegan jams, agave or pure maple syrup. You can store your homemade biscuits in an airtight container in the fridge for up to 4 days.

Southern Crispy Fried Chick'n

Serves 3 or 4

In the South, we love to fry up almost anything, but have you tried oyster mushrooms? You won't miss the chicken once you give these babies a try. These delicious mushrooms are fried in hot oil until golden brown and tender. The result is a satisfying and savory dish perfect for an entrée or by itself with some good ol' dipping sauce. You can even use the chick'n pieces as a topping for salads, sandwiches and pasta dishes. The southern style of frying oyster mushrooms is tasty and an easy way to enjoy one of my favorite mushrooms on the planet! Of course, pairing it with my biscuits in an epic sandwich is my suggestion to start!

Mushrooms

6 to 8 medium-sized to large oyster mushrooms

1 cup (240 ml) avocado oil

Wet Batter

1 cup (125 g) organic all-purpose, unenriched, unbleached flour

1 tsp garlic powder

1 tsp onion powder

1 tsp Louisiana-style Cajun seasoning

1 tsp smoked paprika

1½ cups (355 ml) unflavored, unsweetened oat milk (or any plant-based milk of your choice)

Dry Batter

1 cup (125 g) organic all-purpose, unenriched, unbleached flour

½ tsp smoked paprika

1½ tsp (9 g) sea salt

½ tsp freshly ground black pepper

2 tsp (5 g) Louisiana-style Cajun seasoning

1 tsp adobo powder

1 tsp cornstarch

1 tbsp (2 g) dried parsley

½ cup (45 g) vegan panko bread crumbs

Prepare the mushrooms: Clean the mushrooms with a damp paper towel or a small bristle brush to remove any dirt.

Prepare the wet batter: In a large bowl, combine the flour, garlic powder, onion powder, Cajun seasoning and smoked paprika, and stir well. Add the oat milk and stir until smooth.

Prepare the dry batter: In a separate bowl, add all the dry batter ingredients and mix well until you have a smooth consistency.

In a large, deep skillet over medium heat, heat the avocado oil to 350°F (180°C). Dredge the mushrooms in the wet batter and then the dry batter. Repeat each step one more time to make a crisper coating. Shake off any excess batter and set your dredged mushrooms aside.

Add the mushrooms to the hot oil, cooking only two or three at a time and being sure not to overcrowd your skillet. Fry on each side for 5 to 7 minutes, or until browned and crispy to your liking. Place the fried mushrooms on a cooling rack. Allow to cool for 1 to 2 minutes. Serve while hot.

Soulful Cornbread Muffuletta

Serves 6 to 8

I lived in Louisiana for a few years. I couldn't escape the Mardi Gras beads, the humidity, and most important, the delicious cuisine. One day, in Shreveport, I wandered into Monjunis, a restaurant with a name that's as fun to say as the food is to eat. Now, back then, I wasn't vegan and let's just say I had a personal relationship with big sandwiches. But my life was forever changed when I took my first bite of their epic muffuletta. It was served on a big piece of French bread—a flavor explosion—and I was hooked. Fast-forward to today, when I've embraced the vegan lifestyle, and of course, I couldn't resist putting my own twist on that N'awlins classic. So, here's my take on the muffuletta, a sandwich that's a little bit of Shreveport and a little bit of me.

Vegan Cornbread

Vegan butter, for pan (optional)

1 cup (140 g) organic cornmeal

1 cup (125 g) organic all-purpose, unenriched, unbleached flour

1 tbsp (14 g) baking powder

½ tsp baking soda

½ tsp salt

1 cup (240 ml) unflavored, unsweetened oat milk (or any plant-based milk of your choice)

1 tbsp (15 ml) apple cider vinegar

¼ cup (60 ml) agave or date syrup

¼ cup (60 ml) olive oil

½ cup (55 g) drained, sliced and seeded fresh jalapeño

Muffuletta Filling

2 tbsp (30 ml) olive oil

3 cups (210 g) sliced organic portobello mushrooms or (534 g) drained and chopped canned jackfruit

2 cloves garlic, minced

½ cup (75 g) chopped roasted red bell peppers

½ cup (50 g) sliced green olives

½ cup (50 g) sliced black olives

Sea salt and freshly ground organic black pepper

¼ cup (15 g) chopped fresh parsley

1 tsp chopped mixed fresh herbs (basil, oregano, thyme)

Prepare the cornbread. Preheat your oven to 375°F (190°C) and line six to eight wells of a muffin tin with paper liners or butter it lightly with vegan butter (if using).

In a medium-sized bowl, combine the cornmeal, flour, baking powder, baking soda and salt.

In a small bowl, stir together the oat milk and vinegar. Let sit for a few minutes to curdle. Add the agave and olive oil to the milk mixture. Whisk until well combined. Pour the milk mixture into the flour mixture and mix until just combined. Fold in the sliced jalapeños.

Fill each prepared muffin well about two-thirds full of the cornbread batter. Bake for 18 to 20 minutes, or until the cornbread muffins are golden brown and a toothpick inserted into the center of a muffin comes out clean.

Meanwhile, prepare the muffuletta filling: In a large skillet, heat the olive oil over medium-high heat.

Add the mushrooms to the skillet and sauté until they start to brown and release their moisture. This should take 5 to 7 minutes. Add the garlic to the skillet and sauté for another 1 to 2 minutes until fragrant. Stir in the roasted red bell peppers and continue to cook for an additional 2 to 3 minutes to heat them through. Add the green and black olive slices to the skillet. Sauté for 2 to 3 more minutes, or until they are well mixed with the other ingredients.

Season the mixture with salt and black pepper to taste; remember that olives can be salty, so adjust the salt accordingly. Finally, stir in the parsley and mixed fresh herbs, and cook for an additional minute to incorporate the flavors.

Remove the skillet from heat and let the filling cool slightly.

Slice each cornbread muffin in half horizontally, like a sandwich bun. Spoon a generous portion of the cooked filling onto the bottom half of each muffin. Place the top half of the muffin over the filling to create a sandwich.

The Philly Vegan Cheesesteak

Serves 4

The Philly cheesesteak, beloved by all, has been an iconic classic for ages. But who says you need meat and dairy for an irresistible sandwich? Enter a delicious vegan alternative that's hearty and packed with fresh ingredients. From tender marinated tempeh and mushrooms, to sautéed peppers and onions, all nestled in a crusty roll, this plant-based twist on a Philly favorite is sure to satisfy even the most discerning taste buds. Let's dive into the flavors of Philadelphia with a dish as tasty as it is satisfying!

Tempeh Marinade

3 tbsp (45 ml) coconut liquid aminos or tamari

1 tbsp (15 ml) olive oil

1 tsp smoked paprika

½ tsp garlic powder

½ tsp onion powder

¼ tsp freshly ground black pepper

8 oz (225 g) tempeh, sliced thinly

Caramelized Onions

2 tbsp (30 ml) olive oil

2 large onions, sliced thinly

1 tsp agave syrup (optional)

Sea salt and freshly ground black pepper (optional)

Smoked Portobello Mushrooms

2 tbsp (30 ml) olive oil

2 large portobello mushrooms, cleaned and sliced

1 tsp liquid smoke, or to taste

Sea salt and freshly ground black pepper

For Assembly

4 vegan sub rolls or hoagie buns

Vegan mayonnaise or vegan aioli

Vegan provolone or vegan mozzarella cheese slices

Sliced pickles (optional)

Prepare the tempeh marinade: In a shallow dish, whisk together the coconut liquid aminos, olive oil, smoked paprika, garlic powder, onion powder and pepper. Add the tempeh slices and let marinate for at least 30 minutes, at room temperature, turning occasionally.

Caramelize the onions: In a large skillet, heat the olive oil over medium-low heat. Add the onions and cook them slowly, stirring occasionally, until golden brown and caramelized. This may take 20 to 30 minutes. If using, add the agave plus salt and pepper to taste, for extra flavor.

Prepare the mushrooms: In a separate large skillet, heat the olive oil over medium heat. Add the portobello mushroom slices and drizzle with the liquid smoke. Sauté until the mushrooms become tender and develop a smoky flavor. Season with salt and pepper to taste.

Cook the tempeh: Heat a separate large nonstick skillet or grill pan over medium-high heat. Add the marinated tempeh slices and cook for 2 to 3 minutes per side, or until they are nicely browned and have absorbed the flavors.

To assemble: Split the vegan rolls or buns in half. Spread vegan mayonnaise on one inner side of each roll. Layer the cooked tempeh, caramelized onions and smoked mushrooms on the buns. Top with your vegan cheese slices.

Place the assembled sandwiches under the broiler for 1 to 2 minutes, or until the cheese melts and gets bubbly. Keep a close eye to avoid burning.

Serve these hot. Remove from the broiler and let cool for a minute. If desired, add sliced pickles or other condiments of your choice.

Chick'n Waffle Sammich

Serves 4

Well, butter my waffles and stick something crispy in between! This sammich is mighty special and close to my heart because it combines two of my favorite things: vegan chick'n and delicious waffles. It's a southern twist that will have you saying "Goodness gracious" with every bite. Imagine this, darlin': perfectly crisp and golden waffles infused with cinnamon and cardamom, paired with some crispy chick'n (page 12) that'll make your taste buds do a little electric slide.

1½ cups (188 g) organic all-purpose, unenriched, unbleached flour

2 tsp (9 g) baking powder

½ tsp baking soda

¼ tsp salt

1 tsp ground cinnamon, plus more for sprinkling

½ tsp ground cardamom, plus more for sprinkling

2 tbsp (30 ml) agave syrup

1½ cups (355 ml) unflavored, unsweetened oat milk (or any plant-based milk of your choice)

¼ cup (60 g) applesauce

⅓ cup (76 g) vegan butter, melted

1 tsp vanilla extract

All-purpose baking spray (we prefer La Tourangelle® brand), for waffle iron

Southern Crispy Fried Chick'n (page 12)

In a large bowl, combine the flour, baking powder, baking soda, salt, cinnamon and cardamom. Mix well until evenly distributed.

In a small bowl, whisk together the agave, oat milk, applesauce, vegan butter and vanilla.

Pour the oat milk mixture into the flour mixture and stir until just combined. Be careful not to overmix; a few lumps are okay. Let the batter sit for 5 to 10 minutes, to allow it to thicken slightly.

Preheat your waffle iron according to the manufacturer's instructions. Lightly spray it with all-purpose baking spray, if needed, to prevent sticking. Pour a portion of the batter into the center of the waffle iron, leaving a little space around the edges. Close the lid and cook until the waffles are golden brown and crispy, typically 3 to 5 minutes, depending on your waffle iron.

Carefully remove the waffles from the iron and place them on a plate. Continue with the remaining batter.

Serve these delicious waffles warm, with my Southern Crispy Fried Chick'n (page 12). Or top them with fresh fruit, a drizzle of agave syrup and a sprinkle of extra cinnamon and cardamom, and it's a party in your mouth.

Big Cheezy Burger

Serves 4

Y'all know me and I'm here to tell you this isn't your ordinary burger; it's got a southern kick that will knock your socks off. I'm talking about a burger that's made with beets and lentils and let me tell ya, it's a treat. I was down yonder at True Food Kitchen in Atlanta, Georgia (Buckhead), and I had my first ever beet burger. I've been in love ever since, so I had to make a replica with my own twist.

Beet and Lentil Patties

2 medium-sized beets, peeled

1 cup (198 g) cooked brown lentils

1 cup (115 g) vegan bread crumbs

4 cloves garlic, chopped finely

1 tsp onion powder

1 tsp garlic powder

½ tsp smoked paprika

½ tsp fresh thyme

Salt and freshly ground black pepper

Olive oil, for cooking

For Assembly

4 slices vegan smoked Gouda cheese (I prefer Follow Your Heart® brand)

4 vegan pretzel buns or vegan hamburger buns

½ cup (115 g) vegan mayonnaise or (120 ml) Texas Kickback Sauce (page 147)

2 cups (40 g) fresh arugula

½ cup (72 g) sweet pickles

1 red onion, sliced thinly

1 fresh tomato, sliced thinly

Prepare the patties: Grate the peeled beets and then squeeze out any excess moisture, using a clean kitchen towel or paper towels.

In a large bowl, combine the grated beets, lentils, vegan bread crumbs, garlic, onion powder, garlic powder, paprika and thyme, plus salt and black pepper to taste. Mix everything well until the mixture holds together when pressed. Divide the mixture into four equal portions and shape them into burger patties.

In a large skillet, heat a drizzle of olive oil over medium heat. Once hot, add the patties and cook for 4 to 5 minutes on each side, or until they are browned and crispy on the outside.

In the last minute of cooking, place a slice of vegan cheese on each patty and cover the skillet until the cheese is melted.

While the patties cook, toast the vegan buns until lightly browned. To assemble the burgers, spread the vegan mayonnaise on the bottom half of each toasted bun. Place a patty with melted cheese on each bun, followed by a handful of fresh arugula.

Add a couple of sweet pickles, red onion slices and tomato slices on top of the arugula. Finally, place the warm bun top half on each burger and serve with some good ol' home fries.

Wisconsin Grilled Cheese

Serves 2

A recipe that's cheesy as can be but without a lick of dairy in sight? Yes please. This is going to make you do a little happy dance. Now, I know what you may be thinkin': "Will, how can a grilled cheese be Wisconsin style without real cheese?" Well, it's all about the vegan cheese that you use, the gooey goodness and the comfort only a grilled cheese can bring you.

1 cup (113 g) shredded vegan Cheddar cheese (I prefer Violife® or 365 Whole Foods Market brand)

½ cup (60 g) shredded vegan mozzarella cheese (I prefer Violife or 365 Whole Foods Market brand)

¼ cup (40 g) diced red onion

1 tsp garlic powder

½ tsp smoked paprika

½ tsp freshly ground black pepper

Pinch of salt

2 tbsp (28 g) vegan butter

1 tbsp (15 g) Dijon mustard

2 tbsp (28 g) vegan mayonnaise

4 slices vegan sourdough bread

Chopped fresh chives, for garnish (optional)

In a small bowl, combine the vegan Cheddar and mozzarella, red onion, garlic powder, smoked paprika, pepper and a pinch of salt. Mix well to create the cheese filling.

In another small bowl, mix together the vegan butter, Dijon mustard and vegan mayonnaise to make a creamy spread.

Lay out the sourdough bread slices on a clean surface. On two of the slices, spread the creamy mustard mixture evenly on one side of each slice. Divide the cheese mixture equally between the two slices, spreading it on the other side of each slice. Place the remaining two slices of bread on top of the cheese-covered slices to make two sandwiches.

Heat a large nonstick skillet or griddle over medium heat.

Carefully transfer the sandwiches to the skillet. Grill them for 2 to 4 minutes on each side, or until the bread turns golden brown and crispy and the cheese is melted. Once the sandwiches are cooked to your liking, remove them from the skillet and let cool for a minute.

If desired, sprinkle with fresh chopped chives, for a burst of color and flavor.

Vegan Bacon, Tomato and Avocado Stack

Serves 1

Now, I know we all love a classic BLT! We are putting a little twist and makin' it vegan style! Picture this: You've got those luscious, ripe tomatoes, sizzlin' vegan bacon and creamy avocado all stacking up to create a flavor explosion you won't believe. Whip up this quick sandwich and make your heart and stomach happy! Go ahead and dive into this one now.

8 strips vegan bacon

¼ cup (60 g) vegan mayonnaise

1 tbsp (15 g) Dijon mustard

1 tbsp (15 ml) fresh lemon juice

1 clove garlic, minced

½ tsp smoked paprika

Salt and freshly ground black pepper

4 slices vegan sourdough bread (or vegan gluten-free bread, if preferred)

1 large ripe avocado, peeled, pitted and sliced

2 ripe tomatoes, sliced thinly

Fresh basil leaves, for garnish (optional)

Cook the vegan bacon according to the package instructions until it's nice and crispy. Set it aside on paper towels to remove any excess oil.

Meanwhile, prepare the sauce: In a small bowl, mix together the vegan mayonnaise, Dijon mustard, lemon juice, garlic and smoked paprika, plus salt and pepper to taste. Stir well to combine and adjust the seasoning to your taste.

Toast the vegan bread slices until they're golden brown and crisp.

Now, it's time to build your stacks. Take one slice of the toasted bread and spread a generous layer of the sauce on it. Place a few avocado slices on top of the sauce. Add a layer of sliced tomatoes. Next, add two or three strips of the crispy vegan bacon.

Repeat these layers once more, finishing with the second slice of bread on top. If you're a fan of fresh basil, add a few leaves on top, for a burst of herbal goodness.

Carefully skewer the stack with a toothpick to hold it together. Repeat the process for the remaining slices of bread to create additional stacks.

HAND-HELDS

Whether it's a pretzel (page 31), a corn dog (page 32) or an avocado boat (page 42), this chapter is dedicated to food you can easily hold in your hand, and that's incredibly delicious.

"Veganize Yo'self" BBQ Ribz

Serves 4

Your lips will be smackin', finger-licking will be going on and you'll be wanting more. How can you have ribs without the meat? But let me tell you, we've got a little plant-based magic up our sleeves that's going to have you believing you're at a good ol' southern BBQ joint. These ribs are tender, smoky and slathered with barbecue sauce that will knock your socks off.

Rib Base

1 cup (100 g) vital wheat gluten

¼ cup (30 g) chickpea flour

2 tbsp (16 g) nutritional yeast

1 tsp garlic powder

1 tsp onion powder

½ tsp smoked paprika

½ tsp freshly ground black pepper

½ cup (120 ml) water

2 tbsp (32 g) tomato paste

3 tbsp (45 ml) soy sauce

1 tbsp (15 ml) olive oil

BBQ Sauce

1 cup (240 ml) ketchup

¼ cup (60 ml) apple cider vinegar

¼ cup (60 ml) agave syrup

2 tbsp (19 g) organic coconut sugar or regular sugar

1 tbsp (15 g) Dijon mustard

1 tsp smoked paprika

½ tsp garlic powder

½ tsp onion powder

½ tsp ground cumin

½ tsp chili powder

Salt and freshly ground black pepper

Prepare the rib base: In a medium-sized bowl, combine the vital wheat gluten, chickpea flour, nutritional yeast, garlic powder, onion powder, smoked paprika and black pepper. Mix well.

In a small bowl, whisk together the water, tomato paste, soy sauce and olive oil. Pour the tomato mixture into the wheat gluten mixture and stir to form a dough. Knead the dough for a couple of minutes until it becomes elastic.

Shape the dough into a rectangular slab approximately ½ inch (1.3 cm) thick. Cut the dough into riblike strips, around 1 inch (2.5 cm) wide, and gently stretch them to make them longer.

Prepare a pot of steaming water. Place a steaming basket or colander over it and steam the riblike strips for 30 to 40 minutes, or until firm.

While the rib strips steam, prepare the BBQ sauce: In a medium-sized saucepan, combine the ketchup, vinegar, agave, coconut sugar, Dijon mustard, paprika, garlic powder, onion powder, cumin and chili powder, plus salt and black pepper to taste. Bring to a simmer over medium heat and let cook for 10 to 15 minutes, stirring occasionally. Once the sauce thickens, remove from the heat and set aside.

Preheat your grill to medium-high heat and oil the grates.

Brush the steamed rib strips with a generous amount of BBQ sauce and grill them for 10 to 12 minutes on each side, brushing with more sauce as needed. Grill until they have a nice char and are heated through.

Serve the BBQ ribs with extra BBQ sauce on the side and your favorite vegan coleslaw, cornbread or any other BBQ side dishes you prefer.

Great American Pretzel

Serves 8

Imagine a soft, fluffy pretzel with the perfect golden crust, sprinkled with just the right amount of salt. You'll be pullin' these out of the oven and feelin' like you've stumbled into a small-town fair, right in your own kitchen. Go into the kitchen, grab your apron, get that dough rollin' and prepare yourself to make a vegan pretzel that will have you shoutin' "Y'all, come and get it!"

Pretzel Dough

1½ cups (355 ml) warm water (about 110°F [43°C])

2 tbsp (26 g) organic granulated sugar

2¼ tsp (9 g) active dry yeast

4 cups (500 g) organic all-purpose, unenriched, unbleached flour, plus more for dusting

1½ tsp (9 g) sea salt

Avocado oil or olive oil, for bowl

Everything Topping

1 tsp sesame seeds

1 tsp poppy seeds

1 tsp dried minced garlic

1 tbsp (10 g) dried minced onion

½ tsp flaky sea salt

Prepare the pretzel dough: In a small bowl, combine the warm water and sugar. Sprinkle the yeast over the water and let sit for about 5 minutes, or until it becomes frothy.

In a large bowl, combine the flour and salt. Pour in the yeast mixture and stir until a dough forms. Knead the dough on a floured surface for about 5 minutes, or until smooth and elastic.

Place the dough in an oiled bowl, cover with a clean kitchen towel and let rise for about 1 hour, or until doubled in size.

Preheat your oven to 425°F (220°C) and line a baking sheet with parchment paper.

Prepare the everything topping: In a shallow bowl, combine the sesame seeds, poppy seeds, dried garlic, dried onion and salt.

Punch down the risen dough and divide it into eight equal-sized portions. Roll each portion into a long rope, 20 to 22 inches (51 to 56 cm) long and then form a pretzel shape. Form the rope of dough into a circle with the two ends twisted at the top, leaving a bit of overhang. Pull the twist down on top of the circle, and use the overhang to stick the two ends to the main circle.

Gently brush each pretzel with water and sprinkle them with the everything topping mixture, ensuring they're well coated. Place the pretzels, topping side up, on the prepared baking sheet and bake for 15 to 20 minutes, or until golden brown and cooked through. Pair with my amazing Hot Beer Cheese (page 146).

Love on a Stick: The Corn Dog

Serves 6 to 8

Step right up to a taste of nostalgia with this recipe—a delicious homage to the spirited fairs of Cass County in East Texas. Close your eyes and you'll find yourself strolling down the lanes of the county fair, surrounded by the infectious energy of laughter and the sweet melodies of carnival tunes. Remember those carefree moments when the air was thick with the aroma of tempting treats, and the highlight of the day was sinking your teeth into a warm, golden corn dog? Now, relive those cherished memories with our plant-based twist on this classic fair delight.

1 cup (140 g) cornmeal

1 cup (125 g) organic all-purpose, unenriched, unbleached flour

3 tbsp (39 g) organic granulated sugar

1½ tsp (7 g) baking powder

½ tsp salt

1½ cups (355 ml) unflavored, unsweetened oat milk (or any plant-based milk of your choice)

1 tbsp (15 ml) agave syrup

⅓ cup (80 ml) vegan egg substitute (I prefer JUST Egg® brand)

6 to 8 vegan smoked frankfurters

1 qt (946 ml) coconut or avocado oil, for cooking

Soak six to eight wooden skewers in water for 30 minutes.

Meanwhile, in a large bowl, combine the cornmeal, flour, sugar, baking powder and salt. Next, add the oat milk, agave, vegan egg and 3 tablespoons (45 ml) of the coconut oil to the bowl, reserving the rest of the coconut oil for frying the corn dogs. Mix your batter well, then allow it to rest for 10 to 15 minutes. Meanwhile, cook the vegan smoked frankfurters according to their package directions, then let cool.

Heat your remaining cooking oil to 350°F (180°C).

Pour your batter into a tall drinking glass, filling it almost to the top. Thread a wooden stick through each of the vegan smoked frankfurters, allowing one end of the stick to protrude (to hold onto). Be sure your smoked franks are cool before dipping them. Dip the frankfurters into the batter, making sure to let the excess drip off before frying.

Carefully place the corn dogs in the hot oil, ensuring the entire corn dog is submerged. Fry for 3 to 5 minutes, or until crispy and golden brown.

Transfer your corn dogs to a wire rack to cool. Enjoy with your favorite dipping sauce, such as mustard.

Chi-Town Juicy Slaw Dog

Serves 4 to 6

An old-fashioned hot dog is good, but we're going to kick it up a notch: a juicy vegan sausage of your liking, tucked into a soft bun, topped with the freshest, crunchiest slaw you've ever seen. This is the Chi-town way! If you are looking to try it my way, this recipe's got you covered.

Vegan Slaw

2 cups (180 g) shredded green cabbage

1 cup (90 g) shredded purple cabbage

1 large carrot, julienned

½ red onion, sliced finely

¼ cup (60 g) vegan mayonnaise

1 tbsp (15 g) Dijon mustard

1 tbsp (15 ml) apple cider vinegar

1 tbsp (15 ml) pure maple syrup

Salt and freshly ground black pepper

Special Sauce

¼ cup (60 g) vegan mayonnaise

2 tbsp (30 ml) ketchup

1 tsp pickle relish

½ tsp smoked paprika

½ tsp garlic powder

½ tsp onion powder

Vegan Hot Dogs

4 vegan hot dogs of your choice

4 vegan hot dog buns

Prepare the slaw: In a large bowl, combine the green and purple cabbage, carrot and red onion.

In a small bowl, whisk together the vegan mayonnaise, Dijon mustard, vinegar and maple syrup, plus salt and pepper to taste.

Pour the dressing over the slaw mixture and toss until the vegetables are evenly coated. Refrigerate the slaw for at least 30 minutes to allow the flavors to meld.

Prepare the special sauce: In a small bowl, mix together the vegan mayonnaise, ketchup, pickle relish, smoked paprika, garlic powder and onion powder. Set aside.

Prepare the hot dogs: Grill or panfry your vegan hot dogs, according to the package instructions, until they are heated through and have a nice, slightly crispy exterior. Toast the vegan hot dog buns on the grill or in a toaster until they are lightly browned.

Place a cooked vegan hot dog in each bun. Top each hot dog with a generous serving of the prepared slaw. Drizzle a generous amount of the special sauce over the slaw-topped hot dogs.

Spicy Southwestern Breakfast Burrito

Serves 4

Rise and shine with a kick of flavor in every bite! This recipe invites you to indulge in the hearty traditions of a morning meal that goes beyond the ordinary. The breakfast burrito, a beloved classic, has been the go-to choice for starting the day right. Not only does it promise to fill you up with the robust flavors of the Southwest, but it also embraces the convenience of being freezer-friendly— because who doesn't love a breakfast that can be savored now and later?

Spicy Southwestern Filling

1 tbsp (15 ml) olive oil

1 cup (172 g) cooked black beans, drained

1 cup (150 g) seeded and diced red bell pepper

1 cup (160 g) diced red onion

1 cup (150 g) corn kernels (fresh, frozen or canned and drained)

1 tsp chili powder

½ tsp ground cumin

½ tsp smoked paprika

Salt and freshly ground black pepper

2 to 3 cloves garlic, minced

1 to 2 jalapeño peppers, or to taste, diced finely

Chickpea Scramble

1 (15-oz [425-g]) can chickpeas, drained and rinsed

½ tsp chili powder

½ tsp ground cumin

Salt and freshly ground black pepper

For Assembly

Large flour tortillas

Peeled, pitted and sliced avocado

Fresh cilantro leaves

Lime wedges

Vegan cheese (optional)

Salsa (optional)

Prepare the filling: In a large skillet, heat the olive oil over medium heat. Add the black beans, red bell pepper, red onion and corn kernels. Sauté for about 5 minutes, or until the vegetables start to soften.

Add the chili powder, cumin, smoked paprika, salt and black pepper to taste, garlic and diced jalapeños. Continue to cook for another 5 to 7 minutes, or until the beans are tender and the flavors meld. Adjust the spice level according to your preference.

Prepare the chickpea scramble: In a separate large skillet, mash the chickpeas slightly with a fork or a potato masher.

Season the mashed chickpeas with the chili powder and cumin, plus salt and black pepper to taste. Cook for 5 to 7 minutes, stirring occasionally, until heated through and they have a scrambled egg–like consistency.

Assemble the burritos: Warm the flour tortillas in a dry skillet for a few seconds on each side or microwave them briefly, to make them pliable. Place a generous spoonful of filling down the center of each tortilla. Add a portion of the chickpea scramble on top of the filling.

Top each burrito with avocado slices, cilantro and a squeeze of lime juice. If desired, sprinkle some vegan cheese and salsa on top.

Fold in the sides of the tortilla, then roll it up from the bottom to create a burrito and serve.

Crispy Cajun Potato Wedges

Serves 4

These wedges will have you saying "yee-haw" with every crispy bite. These here potato wedges are a down-home delight that'll make your taste buds do a little jig! Picture this: perfect seasoned russet potatoes, roasted to a golden-brown perfection, with a kick of Cajun spice that'll have your mouth hollerin' for more. They are comfort food at its finest, and it's so easy to make them. I love cooking these taters for breakfast, or I'll even pair them with a meal for dinner. Listen, whenever you want some good ol' country-style taters, this is my go-to recipe.

4 large russet potatoes, skin on, cut into wedges

3 tbsp (45 ml) olive oil

1 tsp onion powder

1 tsp garlic powder

1 tsp dried parsley

2 tsp (5 g) Cajun seasoning

Sea salt

Freshly ground black pepper

Preheat your oven to 425°F (220°C) and line a baking sheet with parchment paper.

In a large bowl, combine the potato wedges with olive oil, ensuring they are evenly coated.

In a small bowl, mix together the onion powder, garlic powder, parsley and Cajun seasoning. Sprinkle the seasoning mixture over the potato wedges, tossing them well to ensure each wedge is coated.

Arrange the seasoned potato wedges in a single layer on the prepared baking sheet, making sure there is space between them, for even crisping. Season with salt and freshly ground black pepper.

Bake for 35 to 40 minutes, or until the wedges are golden brown and crispy. Flip the wedges halfway through the cooking time for even crispiness.

Once done, remove from the oven and let cool for a few minutes before serving these unique crispy Cajun potato wedges as a delicious side dish or snack. They pair well with my Vegan Dipping Sauce (page 48).

Mole Tacos

Serves 8

The enchanting streets of Oaxaca, where the air is filled with the intoxicating aroma of chocolate-infused chili and vibrant colors swirl around you. Now, bring that tapestry of flavors to your kitchen with a plant-based twist on the traditional mole. This velvety, earthy sauce, kissed with the essence of cocoa and the warmth of spices, envelops each morsel in a symphony of taste that's as bold as it is nuanced.

Mole Sauce

2 dried ancho chiles

2 dried guajillo chiles

¼ cup (36 g) raw almonds

¼ cup (35 g) raw pumpkin seeds

¼ cup (35 g) raisins

2 tbsp (30 ml) coconut oil

¼ cup (40 g) chopped onion

2 cloves garlic, minced

1 ripe tomato, chopped

½ tsp ground cinnamon

½ tsp ground cumin

¼ tsp ground cloves

¼ tsp ground allspice

4 oz (113 g) vegan dark chocolate

2 tbsp (30 ml) agave syrup

2 cups (475 ml) vegetable stock

Salt and freshly ground black pepper

For Assembly

8 small corn or flour tortillas

1 cup (185 g) cooked quinoa

1 cup (172) cooked black beans, drained

1 cup diced roasted sweet potatoes

1 cup (5 to 8 oz [140 to 225 g]) sautéed mixed bell peppers and onions

1 cup fresh (20 g) arugula or (30 g) spinach

Lime wedges, for serving

Prepare the mole sauce: Remove and discard the stems and seeds from the dried chiles. Place the chiles in a bowl and cover with boiling water. Let soak for about 20 minutes, or until they become soft.

In a medium-sized, dry skillet, toast the almonds and pumpkin seeds over medium heat until lightly browned. Remove from the skillet and set aside. In the same skillet, toast the raisins for about 2 minutes, or until they plump up, then remove from the skillet and set aside.

In the skillet, heat the coconut oil over medium heat. Add the onion and garlic, and sauté until translucent. Add the tomato, cinnamon, cumin, cloves, allspice, chocolate and agave. Cook until the tomato softens.

Drain the soaked chiles and transfer them to a blender along with the toasted almonds, pumpkin seeds, raisins and the cooked tomato mixture. Blend until smooth, adding vegetable stock as needed to reach your desired consistency. Season with salt and black pepper to taste.

Pour the mole sauce back into the skillet and simmer for 10 to 15 minutes to let the flavors meld. Adjust the seasoning, if needed.

To assemble the tacos, warm the tortillas in a dry skillet or microwave.

Spread a generous spoonful of mole sauce onto a tortilla. Add a layer of cooked quinoa, black beans, roasted sweet potatoes, sautéed bell peppers and onions and fresh arugula. Squeeze a lime wedge over the fillings.

Serve immediately, with any remaining mole sauce on the side for dipping. Enjoy the rich and complex flavors of this unique sauce!

Avocado Boats

Serves 4

Gather your friends for a party and get ready to wow them with these easy and delicious avocado boats. Honey, they're a real healthy southern delight. Creamy avocados, juicy tomatoes and a sprinkle of magical everything topping—it's like a flavor explosion in every bite! I bet you never thought you'd be eating something so delicious that takes less than 10 minutes to make.

2 avocados
1 cup (180 g) diced Roma tomatoes
2 tbsp (18 g) sunflower seeds
2 tbsp (30 ml) coconut liquid aminos
Everything Topping (page 31)
½ cup (17 g) alfalfa sprouts

Cut the avocados in half and remove the pits. Spoon the diced tomato into each avocado half, distributing it evenly among them. Next, add sunflower seeds and coconut liquid aminos to each avocado half.

Generously sprinkle everything topping over the filled avocado boats.

Top each avocado boat with a handful of fresh alfalfa sprouts. This adds a crisp and refreshing element to the dish.

Arrange the filled avocado boats on a serving platter. Drizzle any remaining coconut liquid aminos over the top for added flavor. You can use a spoon to eat these, or pop them out of their hull and use your hands!

Eggplant Bacon?!

Serves 4

This plant-powered alternative re-creates the smoky, savory allure of traditional bacon, but with a compassionate and cruelty-free touch. Thin slices of eggplant marinate in a tantalizing blend of soy sauce, liquid smoke, maple syrup and spices, transforming into crispy, flavorful strips after a turn in the oven. However you serve it, this vegan bacon is a testament to the magic of plant-based creativity.

1 large eggplant
2 tbsp (30 ml) soy sauce or tamari
1 tbsp (15 ml) liquid smoke
1 tbsp (15 ml) pure maple syrup
1 tbsp (15 ml) olive oil
½ tsp smoked paprika
½ tsp garlic powder
¼ tsp freshly ground black pepper
¼ tsp cayenne pepper or to taste
Cooking spray or additional olive oil, for pan

Slice the eggplant lengthwise into thin strips, approximately ⅛ inch (3 mm) thick. You can use a sharp knife or a mandoline slicer for consistent slices.

In a small bowl, whisk together the soy sauce, liquid smoke, maple syrup, olive oil, smoked paprika, garlic powder, black pepper and cayenne.

Place the eggplant slices in a shallow dish and pour the marinade over them, ensuring that each slice is coated evenly. Let marinate at room temperature for at least 30 minutes, or for even better flavor, refrigerate them for a few hours or overnight.

Preheat your oven to 375°F (190°C) and line a baking sheet with parchment paper. You can also lightly spray the parchment paper with cooking spray or oil with a small amount of olive oil. Place the marinated eggplant slices in a single layer on the prepared baking sheet, making sure they don't overlap.

Bake for 20 to 25 minutes, flipping the slices halfway through, or until crispy and slightly browned. Keep a close eye on them, as baking times may vary based on the thickness of your slices.

Remove from the oven and transfer to a wire rack. As they cool, they will become even crispier. Once completely cooled, serve your vegan bacon as a delicious and smoky topping for salads, sandwiches, vegan BLTs or as a crunchy snack on its own.

DIPPERS

I adore appetizers, and this chapter is a personal favorite in this cookbook. These delightful treats can be whipped up quickly, ready to enjoy in no time.

Spicy Fried Half Sours

Serves 4

If you want a dill-licious appetizer that'll have you hollerin' "pickle me this" after the first bite, my half sours are it! I had my first half sour pickles at a bar on Edgewood Street in Atlanta, Georgia, when I lived there, and I can still remember them. The preparation is a breeze—just dip the pickles in a luscious oat milk bath, coat them in a blend of flour, cornmeal and vegan bread crumbs infused with a medley of spices, then fry to a golden perfection in coconut oil. These fried pickles will be a staple when you want a quick fried snack.

Vegan Dipping Sauce

½ cup (115 g) vegan mayonnaise

2 tbsp (30 g) Dijon mustard

1 tbsp (15 ml) pickle juice (from the pickle jar)

½ tsp smoked paprika

½ tsp hot sauce, or to taste

Salt and freshly ground black pepper

Fried Pickles

1 cup (240 ml) unflavored, unsweetened oat milk (or any plant-based milk of your choice)

1 cup (125 g) organic all-purpose, unenriched, unbleached flour

1 cup (140 g) cornmeal

1 cup (90 g) vegan panko bread crumbs

1 tsp paprika

½ tsp garlic powder

½ tsp onion powder

½ tsp freshly ground black pepper

1 (16-oz [455-g]) jar dill pickle slices, drained and patted dry

Coconut oil, for frying

Prepare the dipping sauce: In a small bowl, whisk together the vegan mayonnaise, Dijon mustard, pickle juice, smoked paprika and hot sauce, plus salt and pepper to taste. Taste and adjust the seasonings as needed. Refrigerate the sauce until you're ready to serve.

Prepare the fried pickles: Pour the oat milk into a shallow bowl. In a separate shallow bowl, combine flour, cornmeal, vegan panko, paprika, garlic powder, onion powder and pepper, and mix well.

Take a pickle slice, dip it into the oat milk, allowing any excess to drip off, and then coat it in the flour mixture. Press the coating onto the pickle to ensure it sticks. Place the coated pickle on a baking sheet or tray.

Repeat this process for all pickle slices and then let them rest for 10 to 15 minutes. This allows the coating to set.

In a large, deep skillet, heat about 1 inch (2.5 cm) of coconut oil over medium-high heat. You'll know it's ready when a small piece of breaded pickle sizzles when dropped in.

Carefully add the breaded pickle slices to the hot oil in batches, making sure not to overcrowd the pan. Fry until golden brown and crispy, 2 to 3 minutes per side. Use a slotted spoon to remove the fried pickles and transfer them to a paper towel–lined plate, to drain any excess oil. Repeat the frying process for the remaining pickles.

Serve immediately, alongside the vegan dipping sauce you prepared earlier.

Tomato Fritter Bites

Serves 4

Now, these fritters will have you singing like the Mississippi Mass Choir on a Sunday morning. We're talking about my Southern sensation that have you saying "Good Lawd" after the first bite. I remember my grandmother "Mu" telling us to go to the garden and get some fresh tomatoes so she could fry them up. These 'maters are not just a side dish—they're the star of the show. Now, I love dipping these in my Texas Kickback Sauce (page 147). They are darn good and perfect for any time of the year.

12 (½" [1.3-cm]-thick) slices tomato (from about 4 large tomatoes)

2 tsp (5.5 g) kosher salt

1 cup (125 g) organic all-purpose, unenriched, unbleached flour

½ cup (120 ml) vegan egg substitute (I prefer JUST Egg brand)

1 cup (240 ml) unflavored, unsweetened oat milk (or any plant-based milk of your choice)

1 tsp Tabasco® sauce

2 cups (180 g) Italian-seasoned vegan panko bread crumbs

½ cup (60 g) self-rising yellow cornmeal mix

¼ cup (25 g) grated vegan Parmesan cheese

¼ cup (30 g) grated vegan Cheddar cheese

2 tbsp (19 g) salt-free Creole seasoning (I use Tony Chachere's No Salt Creole Seasoning)

Coconut oil, for frying

Chopped fresh basil, for garnish

Place your tomato slices on a plate and sprinkle with kosher salt on both sides. Allow the tomatoes to sit for 30 minutes, then pat dry with paper towels.

Place the flour in a medium-sized bowl. In a small bowl, whisk together the vegan egg, oat milk and Tabasco sauce. In a separate medium-sized bowl, mix together the panko, cornmeal mix, vegan Parmesan cheese, vegan Cheddar cheese and Creole seasoning.

Working in small batches, dredge each tomato slice in the flour, shaking off any excess. Dip in the vegan egg mixture, allowing any excess to drip off, then coat evenly with the seasoned panko mixture.

In a large, deep skillet, heat the coconut oil over medium-high heat. Fry the tomato fritter bites in batches, 2 to 3 minutes per side, until they are golden brown on both sides. Use a slotted spoon to transfer the fritters to a paper towel–lined plate, to drain any excess oil.

Garnish with chopped fresh basil and serve as a flavorful appetizer or snack.

El Paso Tex-Mex Nachos

Serves 4

Let's head toward the border, but first we shall stop in El Paso. These Tex-Mex nachos will knock your socks off and have you licking your fingers till the last bite. I make these for friends when they come over and they can't stop eating them. You can eat these for lunch or dinner or make them for a party. They're perfect!

Vegan Nacho Cheese Sauce

1 cup (140 g) salted cashews

1 cup (240 ml) hot water (180 to 205°F [82 to 96°C], not boiling)

½ cup (64 g) nutritional yeast

2 tbsp (18 g) pickled jalapeños

2 tbsp (30 ml) pickled jalapeño juice

1 tsp smoked paprika

½ tsp ground cumin

½ tsp garlic powder

¼ tsp sea salt

Freshly ground black pepper, to taste

Nachos

2 tbsp (30 ml) coconut oil

8 oz (225 g) sliced organic mushrooms

Salt and freshly ground black pepper

1 (12-oz [340-g]) bag of your favorite tortilla chips (I like 365 Whole Foods Market Brand blue corn chips)

1 cup (172 g) cooked black beans, drained

1 cup (150 g) cooked corn kernels (fresh, frozen or canned and drained)

½ cup (80 g) diced red onion

½ cup (90 g) diced tomatoes

¼ cup (34 g) pickled jalapeños

¼ cup (4 g) fresh cilantro leaves

Avocado slices or guacamole, for topping

Lime wedges, for garnish

Prepare the cheese sauce: In a blender, preferably a Vitamix®, combine the cashews, water, nutritional yeast, pickled jalapeños, pickled jalapeño juice, smoked paprika, cumin, garlic powder, salt and black pepper.

Blend until the mixture is smooth and creamy. Taste and adjust the seasonings, if necessary. If your cheese sauce has small pieces of nuts in it, continue to blend until creamy and smooth.

Prepare the nachos: In a medium-sized skillet, heat a bit of the coconut oil over medium heat. Add the mushroom slices and sauté until browned and tender, 5 to 7 minutes. Season them with a pinch of salt and black pepper. Set aside.

Preheat your oven to 350°F (180°C).

On a large, oven-safe platter or baking sheet, spread out the tortilla chips in an even layer. Evenly sprinkle the cooked black beans, corn kernels, sautéed mushrooms, diced red onion, tomatoes and the pickled jalapeños over the chips. Drizzle the prepared cheese sauce generously over the chips.

Bake the nachos for 10 to 15 minutes, or until they are heated throughout and the cheese sauce is slightly bubbly. Remove from the oven and garnish with the cilantro leaves.

Add avocado slices or guacamole on top, for a creamy touch.

Serve hot, with lime wedges for extra zing. Enjoy the bold flavors, creamy cheese sauce and the addition of sautéed mushrooms in every bite!

"Hot Dang" Vegan Jalapeño Poppers

Serves 6

These dang jalapeño poppers are what you make when you want to sing "Kumbaya" with a group of friends for a get-together. They're damn good and flavorful with the right amount of spice. They may even make you do a little two-step. These will be a hit for any occasion or just when you are at home chilling by yourself.

1 cup (140 g) raw cashews, soaked in water for 4 hours, then drained

½ cup (28 g) sun-dried tomatoes (not oil-packed), soaked in water for 30 minutes, then drained

¼ cup (32 g) nutritional yeast

2 cloves garlic, minced

1 tbsp (15 ml) fresh lemon juice

1 tsp smoked paprika

½ tsp ground cumin

Salt and freshly ground black pepper

12 large jalapeños, halved and seeded

1 cup (90 g) vegan panko bread crumbs

Fresh cilantro, for garnish

Preheat your oven to 375°F (190°C) and line a baking sheet with parchment paper.

In a food processor, combine the drained cashews and sun-dried tomatoes, nutritional yeast, garlic, lemon juice, smoked paprika and cumin, plus salt and pepper to taste. Process until you achieve a smooth, creamy consistency.

Carefully stuff each jalapeño half with the cashew mixture.

Pour the vegan panko onto a plate. Roll each stuffed jalapeño in the panko, ensuring an even coating. Place the coated jalapeños on the prepared baking sheet and bake for 15 minutes, or until panko turns golden brown and crispy.

Remove from the oven and let cool for a few minutes before serving.

Garnish with fresh cilantro, for an extra burst of flavor. Serve as an appetizer or party snack, and watch them disappear!

Crispy Cajun Mozz Sticks

Serves 4

Well, let the good times roll. That's how they say it in South Louisiana. Brace yourself for a symphony of flavors that will make you feel like you've stepped into the boot! That's slang for the great state of Louisiana. These mozz sticks will have you coming back to make them repeatedly.

2 (8-oz [227-g]) packages Miyoko's Creamery® Vegan Mozzarella, or use 2 (4.65-oz [132-g]) packages Daiya™ brand Cheeze Sticks that are already precut

1 cup (128 g) tapioca starch

1 cup (240 ml) unflavored, unsweetened oat milk (or any plant-based milk of your choice)

1 tbsp (15 ml) apple cider vinegar

1 tbsp (15 ml) hot sauce

1 cup (100 g) oat flour

1 cup (115 g) vegan bread crumbs

½ cup (64 g) nutritional yeast

1 tbsp (7 g) smoked paprika

1 tsp garlic powder

1 tsp onion powder

½ tsp Cajun seasoning

Salt and freshly ground black pepper

High-heat oil, for frying (I prefer coconut or avocado oil)

Cut the mozzarella into sticks. We're letting Miyoko's magic take center stage.

Place the tapioca starch in a shallow bowl.

In a small bowl, whisk together the oat milk, vinegar and hot sauce.

In a medium-sized bowl, mix together the oat flour, vegan bread crumbs, nutritional yeast, smoked paprika, garlic powder, onion powder and Cajun seasoning, plus salt and pepper to taste.

Roll the mozzarella sticks in the tapioca starch, then give them a good dip in the oat milk mixture. Next, coat them generously in the breading mix.

In a large skillet, heat your oil to 375°F (190°C). Work in batches, fry the sticks until they're golden brown and crispy, 2 to 3 minutes per side.

Transfer to rest on some paper towels, to absorb any excess oil.

Plate them up and serve with your favorite vegan marinara sauce. Get ready for a flavor explosion that'll make your taste buds throw a hoedown.

Big Ol' Bloomin' Onion

Serves 4 to 6

We're about to embark on a journey of flavor that'll make you do a little dance in the kitchen. Now, I know we're used to the classic bloomin' onion and we're putting a twist on it—making it vegan and cookin' it up quick in an air fryer. Get ready for a bloomin' good time that's better than your country fair.

Onions

2 large sweet onions

Dry Batter

2½ cups (313 g) organic all-purpose, unenriched, unbleached flour

1 tbsp (7 g) Old Bay® Seasoning

2 tsp (5 g) onion powder

2 tsp (6 g) garlic powder

2 tsp (5 g) paprika

1 tsp freshly ground black pepper

Wet Batter

¾ cup (175 ml) vegan egg substitute (I prefer JUST Egg brand) or (184 g) applesauce

½ cup (120 ml) beer (use your favorite vegan variety)

Avocado or olive oil spray

Texas Kickback Sauce (page 147)

Set an air fryer to 400°F (200°C) and let it preheat while you prepare the bloomin' onions.

Prep the onions: Peel and trim the onions, leaving the root intact. Cut about ½ inch (1.3 cm) from the top of each onion, then make eight vertical cuts, without cutting through the root, to create "petals."

Prepare the dry batter: In a large bowl, combine all of the dry batter ingredients and mix well to ensure even seasoning.

Prepare the wet batter: In a small bowl, whisk together the vegan egg and beer until well combined.

Take each onion and dredge it first in the dry batter, making sure to get the mixture between the "petals." Then, dip it into the wet coating, ensuring it's well-coated. For a thicker batter, repeat this step. Lightly spray each coated onion with canola or olive oil. This will help achieve that golden crispiness we all love.

Place the coated onions in the air fryer basket, ensuring they are not touching. Cook for 12 to 14 minutes, or until golden brown and crispy. You might want to flip them halfway through, for even cooking.

Once they're hot and crispy, remove the onions from the air fryer. Serve them up on a platter with your favorite vegan dipping sauce—I prefer my Texas kickback sauce—if you fancy.

SOUTHERN COMFORT EATS

You already know this chapter is near and dear to my heart! Let's dive into the tastes of the South—the ones I grew up with and the ones that define family for me. No one does street food like the South!

Hoppin' John the Vegan Way

Serves 4

Growing up, the aroma of southern comfort filled my kitchen, creating cherished memories that lingered like a familiar melody. This recipe is a plant-based twist on a southern classic, capturing the heartiness and soulful essence of the dish in every flavorful bite. This dish invites you to savor a medley of black-eyed peas, rice and a symphony of aromatic spices. Each spoonful is a journey through robust textures and a tapestry of rich tastes that pay homage to tradition while embracing the vibrant essence of plant-based living.

1 cup (185 g) dried black-eyed peas, soaked in water overnight, then drained

2 cups (475 ml) vegetable stock

1 cup (195 g) uncooked long-grain white rice

1 tbsp (15 ml) olive oil

1 medium-sized onion, chopped finely

2 cloves garlic, minced

1 green bell pepper, seeded and diced

1 celery rib, diced

1 tsp smoked paprika

½ tsp dried thyme

½ tsp cayenne pepper, or to taste

Salt and freshly ground black pepper

1 (14-oz [400-g]) can diced tomatoes, undrained

3 green onions, chopped, for garnish

Chopped fresh parsley, for garnish

In a medium-sized saucepan, combine the drained black-eyed peas and vegetable stock. Bring to a boil over high heat, then lower the heat to low and simmer until the peas are tender, 30 to 40 minutes.

Meanwhile, cook the rice according to the package instructions.

In a large skillet, heat the olive oil over medium heat. Add the onion, garlic, green bell pepper and celery. Sauté until the vegetables are tender, about 5 minutes.

Add to the skillet the smoked paprika, thyme and cayenne, plus salt and black pepper to taste. Stir to combine. Pour in the diced tomatoes with their juice. Bring the mixture to a simmer and let cook for an additional 10 minutes.

Once the black-eyed peas are tender, drain away any excess liquid and add them to the skillet. Stir to combine with the vegetable mixture. Adjust the seasonings to taste and let the hoppin' John simmer for an additional 5 to 10 minutes, allowing the flavors to meld.

Serve the hoppin' John over a bed of the cooked rice. Garnish with chopped green onions and fresh parsley.

Mardi Gras Mac & Cheese

Serves 6

Laissez les bons temps rouler, y'all! Now, if you're not familiar with the phrase, it's Cajun French for "Let the good times roll." Inspired by the lively culture down in N'awlins, I present to you a true celebration of taste and tradition. Picture this: the vibrant colors of parade floats, the lively tunes of jazz and the unmistakable aroma of Cajun spices. This isn't your ordinary mac & cheese—it's a flavorful fiesta, a Mardi Gras bash on your taste buds. So, grab a spatula, let the good times roll and indulge in the soulful goodness of the South right at your table!

1 tbsp (15 ml) grapeseed oil

⅓ cup (53 g) finely minced onion

3 cloves garlic, finely minced

1½ tsp (9 g) sea salt, divided

3 vegan sausages, diagonally sliced in ½" (1.3-cm) pieces

16 oz (455 g) dried elbow macaroni or other pasta, cooked according to package instructions, ¼ cup (60 ml) cooking water reserved

1 (8-oz [227-g]) package vegan Cheddar shreds

1 (8-oz [227-g]) package vegan mozzarella cheese

½ cup (114 g) vegan butter

¼ cup (32 g) nutritional yeast

2 tsp (5 g) Cajun seasoning

1 tbsp (7 g) onion powder

1 tsp garlic powder

1 (4-oz [113-g]) container fresh vegan Parmesan cheese

1½ tsp (3 g) freshly ground black pepper

Heat a medium-sized skillet over medium-high heat and add the grapeseed oil. Add the onion, garlic and ½ teaspoon of the salt, and sauté until slightly translucent. Add the vegan sausage slices, lower the heat to medium and continue to cook for about 5 minutes, stirring occasionally with a wooden spoon until the exterior of the sausage starts to turn golden brown. Turn off the heat and set aside.

Transfer the cooked macaroni to a 10 x 12-inch (25 x 30-cm) baking pan. Add the vegan sausage mixture and spread it out evenly on top of the cooked macaroni.

In a large saucepan, heat the reserved pasta water on medium-high. Add the vegan Cheddar shreds, vegan mozzarella, vegan butter, nutritional yeast, Cajun seasoning, onion powder, garlic powder and remaining teaspoon of salt. Cook the mixture for 7 to 10 minutes, stirring often with a wooden spoon, breaking down bits of cheese, until the cheese sauce has a smooth and creamy texture.

Remove from the heat and add the cheese sauce to the baking pan along with the vegan sausage mixture. Mix well to completely cover the pasta with the cheese sauce. Top evenly with the vegan Parmesan and pepper.

Heat your oven broiler to medium-high. Broil the mac & cheese for 1 to 2 minutes, or until the top is golden. Remove from the oven and serve!

Texas Sausage Kolaches

Serves 12

One of my fondest memories from growing up in Texas is indulging in the savory delight of traditional kolaches. You can find shops all throughout East Texas that sell these delicacies. Those warm, pillowy pastries filled with a burst of flavors were a breakfast staple. Re-creating the magic with a vegan twist, I've crafted this recipe that captures the essence of my Texas roots.

Kolaches

1 cup (240 ml) unflavored, unsweetened oat milk (or any plant-based milk of your choice), warm (about 110°F [43°C])

¼ cup (50 g) organic granulated sugar

2¼ tsp (9 g) active dry yeast

4 cups (500 g) organic all-purpose, unenriched, unbleached flour, plus more for dusting

½ tsp salt

½ cup (114 g) vegan butter, melted

Vegan butter, at room temperature, for bowl and pan

12 vegan sausage links, cooked ahead according to package instructions

Topping

¼ cup (57 g) vegan butter, melted

1 tbsp (15 ml) pure maple or agave syrup

Prepare the kolaches: In a small bowl, combine the warm oat milk, sugar and yeast. Let sit for about 5 minutes, or until frothy.

In a large bowl, combine the flour and salt. Pour the yeast mixture and melted vegan butter into the flour mixture. Stir until a dough forms.

Knead the dough on a floured surface for 5 to 7 minutes, or until smooth. Butter a bowl with vegan butter. Place the dough in the prepared bowl, cover and let rise for 1 hour, or until doubled in size.

Preheat your oven to 375°F (190°C).

Punch down the risen dough and divide it into 12 equal portions. Roll each portion into a ball and flatten it into a disk.

Place a cooked vegan sausage link in the center of each dough disk. Fold the edges of the dough over the sausage, pinching to seal. Butter a baking sheet with vegan butter or line it with parchment paper. Arrange the kolaches on the prepared baking sheet. Bake for 20 to 25 minutes, or until the kolaches are golden brown.

While the kolaches bake, prepare the topping: In a small bowl, mix together the melted vegan butter and maple syrup. Brush the warm kolaches with the buttery syrup mixture right after taking them out of the oven.

Let the kolaches cool slightly before serving.

Earl's Frito Pie

Serves 4

Saddle up for a taste of East Texas that'll make your taste buds jump with joy! My dad, Willie Earl, makes the best Frito pie. And I had to do him an honor and veganize it. We're rustlin' up something special—my East Texas version of this, a dish so downright delightful it'll have you hollerin' for seconds. Picture this: savory mushrooms, onions and that Texas chili seasoning comin' together in a dance of flavors. So, grab a fork and get ready for a flavor rodeo that'll leave you sayin' "Y'all, that's some mighty fine eatin'!"

2 tbsp (30 ml) olive oil

1 onion, chopped

2 tbsp (20 g) minced garlic

3 to 4 (210 to 280 g) cups finely chopped organic portobello mushrooms

1 cup (260 g) fire-roasted tomatoes

1 cup (150 g) canned whole-kernel corn, drained

1 (1.2-oz [34-g]) package Texas chili seasoning (we use Fire & Smoke Society® brand Chili Seasoning)

Vegan corn chips, for serving (I prefer Fritos®)

Vegan Nacho Cheese Sauce (page 52)

1 cup (180 g) chopped Roma tomatoes, for topping

Sliced jalapeños, for topping

Chopped fresh cilantro, for topping (optional)

In a large skillet, heat the olive oil over medium-high heat. Add the onion and garlic, and sauté for 6 to 8 minutes, or until they begin to soften.

Next, add the chopped mushrooms, fire-roasted tomatoes, corn and the Texas chili seasoning to the skillet. Cook for 12 to 15 minutes, allowing the mushrooms to cook down and the flavors to meld into a hearty chili.

Plate by placing vegan corn chips at the base of a bowl. Ladle the warm mushroom chili over the corn chips, creating a flavorful foundation for your frito pie.

For the finishing touch, generously drizzle your homemade cheese sauce over the mushroom chili, then sprinkle the chopped tomatoes, sliced jalapeños and chopped cilantro (if using) on top of the pie.

Mushroom Fingers

Serves 4

Indulge in the delightful crunch and earthy flavor of these vegan mushroom fingers—sliced portobello mushrooms coated in golden panko crumbs, deep-fried in nourishing coconut oil—a truly irresistible and satisfying appetizer. These babies are simple to make and delicious. Cook these up for a light snack or for a party.

1 cup (240 ml) unsweetened coconut oil, for frying

1 cup (90 g) vegan panko bread crumbs

1 cup (125 g) organic all-purpose, unenriched, unbleached flour

1 tsp garlic powder

1 tsp onion powder

1 tsp smoked paprika

½ tsp salt

¼ tsp freshly ground black pepper

4 large organic portobello mushrooms, cleaned and sliced into finger-sized strips

Vegan dipping sauce of choice (I prefer my Texas Kickback Sauce, page 147)

In a deep fryer or large, deep skillet heat the coconut oil to 350°F (180°C).

In a shallow bowl, combine the vegan panko, flour, garlic powder, onion powder, smoked paprika, salt and pepper. Mix well.

Thoroughly coat each portobello finger in the panko mixture, ensuring an even and generous coating.

Carefully place the coated mushroom fingers into the hot coconut oil, frying in batches to avoid overcrowding. Fry for 2 to 3 minutes, or until golden brown and crispy.

Use a slotted spoon to remove the mushroom fingers from the oil, allowing any excess oil to drain, then transfer them to a paper towel-lined plate to absorb any remaining oil.

Serve immediately with your favorite vegan dipping sauce.

BBQ Skrimps and Grits

Serves 4

In a Southern kitchen, where the symphony of sizzling barbecued shrimp and the comforting allure of grits resonated, these two staples were more than mere ingredients; they were a cherished tradition. Now, let's dive into my vegan twist, starring king oyster mushrooms sliced into shrimplike pieces. Here, grits aren't just a breakfast side; they're an integral part of the entrée, bringing a touch of Southern warmth and tradition to every delightful bite.

4 cups (946 ml) vegetable stock

1 cup (240 ml) unflavored, unsweetened oat milk (or any plant-based milk of your choice)

1 cup (90 g) uncooked stone-ground grits

½ cup (58 g) shredded vegan Cheddar cheese

⅓ cup (77 g) vegan cream cheese

2 tbsp (28 g) vegan butter

Salt and freshly ground black pepper

2 cups (140 g) organic king oyster mushrooms stems, cleaned and sliced into shrimplike shapes

2 tbsp (30 ml) olive oil

1 tbsp (7 g) smoked paprika

1 tsp garlic powder

1 tsp onion powder

½ tsp cayenne pepper (optional)

1 cup (240 ml) BBQ Sauce (page 28)

Chopped fresh parsley, for garnish

Lemon wedges, for serving

In a large saucepan, bring the vegetable stock and oat milk to a boil over high heat. Whisk in the grits, lower the heat to low and simmer until creamy. Stir in the vegan Cheddar cheese, vegan cream cheese and vegan butter, plus salt and black pepper to taste. Turn off the heat and keep warm until serving.

In a medium-sized bowl, combine sliced mushrooms with the olive oil, smoked paprika, garlic powder, onion powder and cayenne (if using).

Heat a grill pan or medium-sized skillet over medium-high heat. Grill the mushrooms for 3 to 4 minutes on each side, or until they develop a slight char, then set aside.

In a small saucepan, heat the BBQ sauce.

Serve the skrimps over the creamy grits, drizzle with BBQ sauce and garnish with fresh parsley. Squeeze the lemon wedges over all before serving.

NORTHERN TREATS

Immerse yourself in the tastes of the North—from savory classics to hearty, carb-filled favorites. These recipes celebrate the culinary treasures of the colder part of the world.

Slappin' Seattle Sesame Ramen

Serves 4

We're fixin' up somethin' special—a vegan ramen that's going to make your body feel good inside and outside. I was in Seattle, Washington, in 2019 and had the best ramen of my life. The restaurant's name is Ramen Danbo, to be exact. So, I had to mimic what I tasted! Now, don't be fooled; just 'cause it's plant-based doesn't mean it lacks flavor. We're going to bring together the heartiness of mushrooms, the richness of peanut butter and the warmth of sesame to create a bowl of comfort.

Ramen

3 tbsp (45 ml) sesame oil, divided

1 cup (160 g) thinly sliced shallots

6 cloves garlic, chopped

8 cups (1.9 L) vegetable stock

3 tbsp (54 g) vegan vegetable bouillon paste

½ cup (128 g) creamy peanut butter

2 tsp (5 g) onion powder, divided

2 tsp (6 g) garlic powder, divided

1 tsp sesame seeds

½ cup (120 ml) coconut liquid aminos, divided

6 cups (420 g) organic baby bella mushrooms

⅓ tsp kosher salt

1 (8-oz [224-g]) packages ramen (I prefer Simply Asia® brand Japanese Style Ramen Noodles)

2 lime leaves

1 tsp chili paste

Toppings

Sprouts

Sliced green onions

Seaweed

Fried chili paste

Shredded carrots

Microgreens

Sesame seeds

Prepare the ramen: In a large pot, heat 1 tablespoon (15 ml) the sesame oil over medium heat. Sauté the shallots and garlic until translucent and slightly caramelized. Add the vegetable stock and vegetable bouillon paste to the pot. Simmer for about 10 minutes, to allow the flavors to meld together.

In a small bowl, combine the peanut butter, 1 teaspoon of onion powder, 1 teaspoon of garlic powder, sesame seeds and ¼ cup (60 ml) of the coconut liquid aminos. Stir well to remove any chunks.

In a large skillet, heat the remaining 2 tablespoons (30 ml) of sesame oil over medium heat, then add the mushrooms, remaining onion powder, remaining garlic powder, salt and remaining ¼ cup (60 ml) of coconut liquid aminos. Cook for about 5 minutes, or until the mushrooms soften and there's no liquid remaining from mushrooms. Remove from the heat and set aside; you will add these, sliced, at the end as a topping.

Add your ramen noodles to the pot of broth and cook according to the package directions. Add the lime leaves for a more robust flavor.

Stir the peanut butter mixture into the pot until fully incorporated. Let the soup simmer for an additional 5 minutes. Add the chili paste to the pot. Stir well and cook for another 5 minutes, to infuse the flavors.

Divide the cooked ramen noodles among four bowls. Ladle the hot soup over the noodles, ensuring each bowl gets an equal amount of broth and shallots.

Top each bowl with sliced mushrooms, sprouts, green onions, seaweed, fried chili paste, shredded carrots, microgreens and sesame seeds, according to your preference.

"Aye, Calzone! I'm Walking Here!"

Serves 4

One night, after leaving a party in Atlanta, I was hungry. Everyone was raving about this pizza parlor, and I had to check out the calzones. And it was a hit! So, here's my version of that delicious night in ATL. I know what you're thinking? Calzone, in Atlanta? Yes, trust me; the "South" has taken inspiration from the North to heart. And the calzones at Fellini's will give any Chicago and New York pizza parlor a run for its money. This calzone brings together the goodness of spinach, artichokes and a touch of southern love. It's a hug for your belly and I guarantee you'll be sayin' "Give me some more!"

Dough

1½ cups (355 ml) warm water (about 110°F [43°C])

1 tbsp (13 g) organic granulated sugar

2¼ tsp (9 g) active dry yeast

4 cups (500 g) organic all-purpose, unenriched, unbleached flour, plus more for dusting

1 tsp sea salt

2 tbsp (30 ml) olive oil

Coconut oil, for bowl

Filling

2 cups (60 g) fresh spinach, chopped

1 (14-oz [400-g]) can artichoke hearts, drained and chopped

1½ cups (173 g) shredded vegan mozzarella

½ cup (115 g) vegan cream cheese

¼ cup (32 g) nutritional yeast

4 cloves garlic, minced

Salt and freshly ground black pepper

Toppings

¼ cup (60 ml) olive oil

1 tbsp (3 g) dried oregano

1 tbsp (8 g) sesame seeds

Marinara sauce, for dipping

Prepare the dough: In a small bowl, combine the warm water, sugar and yeast. Let sit for about 5 minutes, or until frothy.

In a large bowl, mix together the flour and salt. Create a well in the center, then pour in the yeast mixture and olive oil. Knead the dough on a floured surface for 5 to 7 minutes, or until smooth and elastic.

Place the dough in a coconut oil–greased bowl, cover it and let rise for about 1 hour, or until doubled in size.

Prepare the filling: In a medium-sized bowl, combine the spinach, artichoke hearts, vegan mozzarella, vegan cream cheese, nutritional yeast and garlic, plus salt and pepper to taste. Mix well.

Preheat your oven to 425°F (220°C).

Divide the dough into four equal portions. Roll each portion into a ball and then flatten it into a round disk on a floured surface.

Spoon the filling onto one-half of each dough disk, leaving a bare border around the edges. Fold the other half of the dough over the filling, forming a half-moon shape. Press the edges together, to seal.

Transfer the calzones to a baking sheet lined with parchment paper. Brush the tops with the olive oil and sprinkle with the oregano and sesame seeds. Bake for 20 to 25 minutes, or until the calzones are golden brown and cooked through. Serve with marinara sauce.

Oh! My . . . Buffalo Cauliflower Wangs

Serves 4

Let's throw down a twist on the classic—Buffalo wings! Now, I know you might be used to them chicken wings, but let me tell you, these cauliflower wangs are going to make you forget about chicken. Yep, I said it! They're crispy, they're spicy and they're so good. Whip these up for a party or make them for a movie night. Whatever the occasion, they will be a hit.

Cauliflower

1 cup (125 g) organic all-purpose, unenriched, unbleached flour

1 cup (240 ml) unflavored, unsweetened oat milk (or any plant-based milk of your choice)

2 tsp (6 g) garlic powder

2 tsp (2 g) onion powder

½ tsp smoked paprika

½ tsp freshly ground black pepper

¼ tsp cayenne pepper, or to taste

1 cup (90 g) vegan panko bread crumbs

1 large head cauliflower, cut into florets

Buffalo Sauce

½ cup (120 ml) hot sauce (such as Frank's RedHot® brand)

¼ cup (57 g) vegan butter, melted

1 tbsp (15 ml) agave syrup

1 tsp garlic powder

½ tsp onion powder

Sea salt

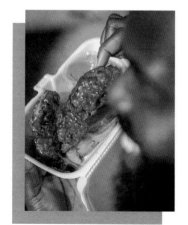

Prepare the cauliflower: Preheat your oven to 450°F (230°C). Line a baking sheet with parchment paper.

In a large bowl, whisk together the flour, oat milk, garlic powder, onion powder, smoked paprika, black pepper and cayenne to create a batter. Place the panko in a separate bowl.

Dip each cauliflower floret into the batter, ensuring it's well coated, then roll it in the panko, pressing gently to adhere.

Place the coated cauliflower in a single layer on the prepared baking sheet. Bake for 20 to 25 minutes, or until golden brown and crispy.

Meanwhile, prepare the Buffalo sauce: In a small saucepan over low heat, combine the hot sauce, melted vegan butter, agave syrup, garlic powder, onion powder and salt. Stir until the butter is melted and the sauce is well combined. Add more hot sauce, if desired, to adjust the heat level to your preference.

Once the cauliflower is done baking, transfer it to a large bowl. Pour the Buffalo sauce over the cauliflower and toss until each piece is coated evenly.

Maple Mustard Vegan Tater Hot Dish

Serves 6

You might be wonderin' what in the world a hot dish is—it's a hug on a plate, that's what it is! This here recipe is a flavor dance between sweet maple, zesty mustard and those crispy tot-style potatoes. It's so good, you'll be saying "Sho'nuff, that's tasty!"

1¼ tbsp (19 ml) olive oil

1 large red onion, chopped finely

3 cloves garlic, minced

1 lb (455 g) vegan ground beef substitute (soy crumbles or organic mushroom)

1 (15-oz [425-g]) can mixed vegetables, drained

1 (10.5-oz [310-ml]) can vegan cream of mushroom soup (I prefer Amy's® brand)

¼ cup (60 ml) pure maple syrup

2 tbsp (30 g) Dijon mustard

Sea salt and freshly ground black pepper

Avocado oil or olive oil spray, for baking dish

1 (24-oz [680-g]) bag frozen vegan tot-style potatoes

1 cup (113 g) vegan shredded Cheddar cheese (I prefer Violife brand)

Chopped fresh parsley, for garnish

Preheat your oven to 375°F (190°C).

In a large skillet, heat the olive oil over medium heat. Add the red onion and sauté until translucent, 3 to 4 minutes. Add the garlic and vegan ground beef substitute. Cook until the vegan meat is browned, 6 to 8 minutes.

To the same skillet, add the mixed vegetables, vegan cream of mushroom soup, maple syrup and Dijon mustard, plus salt and pepper to taste. Stir well to combine, ensuring the mixture is evenly coated.

Spray a baking dish with avocado oil or olive oil. Transfer the mixture to the prepared baking dish. Arrange the frozen tots on top in an even layer, covering the entire dish.

Bake for 30 minutes. After 30 minutes, sprinkle the vegan Cheddar cheese over the top, then bake for an additional 15 minutes, or until the tots are golden brown and crispy and the cheese is melted and bubbly.

Remove from the oven and let cool for a few minutes. Garnish with chopped fresh parsley and serve.

Vegan Canadian Bacon and Cheddar Biscuits

Serves 12

Step into a world where the aroma of freshly baked biscuits envelops your kitchen like a warm, comforting hug. These golden-brown biscuits are generously studded with savory bacon bits and oozing with melted vegan Cheddar. I love making these for my partner, Austyn; he can't get enough of them.

1 cup (240 ml) unflavored, unsweetened oat milk (or any plant-based milk of your choice)

1 tbsp (15 ml) apple cider vinegar

2 cups (250 g) organic all-purpose, unenriched, unbleached flour, plus more for dusting

1 tbsp (14 g) baking powder

½ tsp baking soda

½ tsp salt

½ cup (114 g) vegan butter, cold and cubed

1 cup (113 g) shredded vegan Cheddar cheese

½ cup (56 g) vegan bacon bits (made from tempeh or your preferred plant-based option)

1 tbsp (15 ml) pure maple syrup

Vegan butter, at room temperature, for brushing

Preheat your oven to 425°F (220°C). Line a baking sheet with parchment paper.

In a small bowl, combine the oat milk and vinegar. Let sit for a few minutes to curdle, to create a vegan buttermilk.

In a large bowl, whisk together the flour, baking powder, baking soda and salt. Add cold, cubed vegan butter to the flour mixture. Using a pastry cutter or your fingers, work the butter into the flour until it resembles coarse crumbs.

Mix in the vegan Cheddar cheese and vegan bacon bits, ensuring even distribution.

Pour in the vegan buttermilk and maple syrup. Stir until just combined; do not overmix.

Turn out the dough onto a floured surface. Pat it down to about a 1-inch (2.5-cm) thickness. Use a round biscuit cutter to cut out 12 biscuits. Place them on the prepared baking sheet.

Bake for 12 to 15 minutes, or until golden brown. Remove from the oven. While still warm, brush the tops of the biscuits with vegan butter.

The Northern Neighbor Skewers

Serves 4

Grilled to perfection, these tempeh skewers are not just a meal; they're an experience, an exploration of taste and texture that will leave you craving plant-based perfection. Get ready to elevate your grilling game and indulge in the delightful world this true celebration of vibrant, cruelty-free flavors! In Atlanta, there's a street food market by the name of Krog Street Market, and inside it, a restaurant called Yalla! has some delicious eats. These skewers are a combination of the flavors from the bright eatery that serves Middle Eastern food, and takes a nod of inspiration from the skewers served at NYC food trucks.

¼ cup (60 ml) pure maple syrup

3 tbsp (45 g) Dijon mustard

2 tbsp (30 ml) coconut liquid aminos

2 tbsp (30 ml) apple cider vinegar

4 cloves garlic, minced

1 tsp smoked paprika

1 tsp onion powder

½ tsp freshly ground black pepper

2 (1-lb [455-g]) packages tempeh

Bell peppers, cherry tomatoes, red onions (or vegetables of your choice), cut into chunks

---

Soak four wooden skewers in water for 20 minutes.

In a small bowl, whisk together the maple syrup, Dijon mustard, coconut liquid aminos, vinegar, garlic, smoked paprika, onion powder and pepper until well combined. Taste and adjust the sweetness or saltiness to your liking.

Cut the tempeh into bite-sized cubes and place them in a shallow dish. Pour half of the maple syrup mixture over the tempeh, ensuring each piece is well coated. Reserve the remaining mixture for basting and dipping.

Let the tempeh marinate at room temperature for at least 30 minutes, or for an even richer flavor, refrigerate for a few hours or overnight.

Preheat your grill or grill pan.

Thread the marinated tempeh cubes and vegetable chunks onto the soaked wooden skewers, alternating between tempeh and veggies. Discard the used marinade. Place the skewers on the preheated grill over medium to high heat and cook for 10 to 15 minutes, turning occasionally and basting with the reserved maple syrup mixture.

Once the tempeh is golden brown and the vegetables are tender, remove the skewers from the heat and serve.

FOODIE GLOBE-TROTTING

Take a culinary journey across the globe with my own twist on beloved dishes. Packed with flavor and designed for anyone to re-create, this chapter is a global exploration in your kitchen. We'll explore street foods from around the world— every culture and country has its treasure trove, and now you can enjoy them all in your kitchen!

Elotes

Serves 4 to 6

In the heart of Southern kitchens, the harmonious blend of Tex-Mex spices and Southern comfort food reigns supreme. My culinary journey through vibrant street food cultures, both in Texas and beyond, have inspired the magic that happens when these flavors come together. These *elotes* capture this essence—a combo of creamy textures, smoky notes and a burst of lime. It's my ode to the rich cultural connections in the world of street food. Pop those corn cobs in the fridge and voilà, you've got a flavor-packed companion for your gatherings that lasts a solid four days.

4 to 6 ears corn, husked

½ cup (113 g) vegan mayonnaise

½ cup (115 g) vegan sour cream or Mexican crema

⅓ cup (5 g) finely chopped cilantro leaves, plus more for serving

1 (0.8-oz [23-g]) package elote corn seasoning (I prefer Fire & Smoke Society brand), divided

⅓ cup (38 g) crumbled vegan mozzarella cheese (I prefer Violife brand)

1 tsp smoked paprika

1 lime, cut into wedges

Set your grill to medium heat. Grill the corn until lightly charred on all sides, about 10 to 12 minutes. Cover to keep warm.

In a wide, shallow bowl, whisk together the vegan mayonnaise, vegan sour cream, cilantro and corn seasoning to taste.

Place each ear of grilled corn in the mayonnaise mixture, rolling the cob until evenly coated.

Serve warm or at room temperature, topped with vegan mozzarella, cilantro, a pinch of corn seasoning, the smoked paprika and lime wedges.

All A-Banh Mi (Suki Banh Mi)

Serves 4

The first time I had a *banh mi* was in 2012 in East Atlanta Village. The place was named We Suki Suki and that sammich changed my life. This sammich is double-battered soy curls that dance with Southern spices, nestled in a crusty baguette and harmonizing with pickled veggies and creamy Sriracha mayonnaise. You'll be making this for the rest of your life.

Pickled Veggies
½ cup (120 ml) rice vinegar

¼ cup (50 g) organic granulated sugar

1 tsp salt

1 large carrot, julienned

1 daikon radish, julienned

Sweet Spicy Sriracha Mayo
½ cup (115 g) vegan mayonnaise

2 tbsp (30 ml) Sriracha

¼ cup (60 ml) agave syrup

1 tbsp (15 ml) fresh lime juice

Crispy Soy Curls
2 cups (80 g) soy curls

1 cup (240 ml) unflavored, unsweetened oat milk (or any plant-based milk of your choice)

1 cup (125 g) organic all-purpose, unenriched, unbleached flour

1 cup (90 g) vegan panko bread crumbs

1 tbsp (8 g) Cajun seasoning

1 tsp garlic powder

1 tsp onion powder

Salt and freshly ground black pepper

Coconut oil or avocado oil, for frying

Banh Mi
4 vegan baguettes

Pickled veggies

Fresh cilantro

Sliced jalapeño

Prepare the pickled veggies: In a medium-sized bowl, mix together the rice vinegar, sugar and salt until the sugar dissolves. Add the julienned carrot and daikon radish, ensuring they're fully submerged. Let it sit for at least 20 minutes.

Prepare the Sriracha mayo: In a small bowl, whisk together the vegan mayonnaise, Sriracha, agave and lime juice. Adjust the heat to your liking.

Prepare the soy curls: Rehydrate the soy curls according to the package instructions. Pour the oat milk into a small bowl. In a separate shallow bowl, mix together the flour, vegan panko, Cajun seasoning, garlic powder, onion powder, and salt and pepper to taste.

Dip the soy curls into the oat milk and then coat them in the flour mixture, repeating both steps for a double batter.

Heat the coconut oil in a skillet and fry the soy curls for 5 to 7 minutes, until golden brown and crispy. Transfer the soy curls to paper towels to drain any excess oil.

Assemble the banh mi: Slice the baguettes horizontally without cutting all the way through them, to make a hinged roll. Slather each cut side with the Sriracha mayonnaise. Place a generous amount of crispy soy curls on the bottom half of each roll. Top with the pickled veggies you made earlier, cilantro leaves and sliced jalapeño. Close each sandwich and press it down gently.

Cut your banh mi into halves or thirds, depending on your preference. Serve with a side of a little extra Sriracha mayonnaise for dipping.

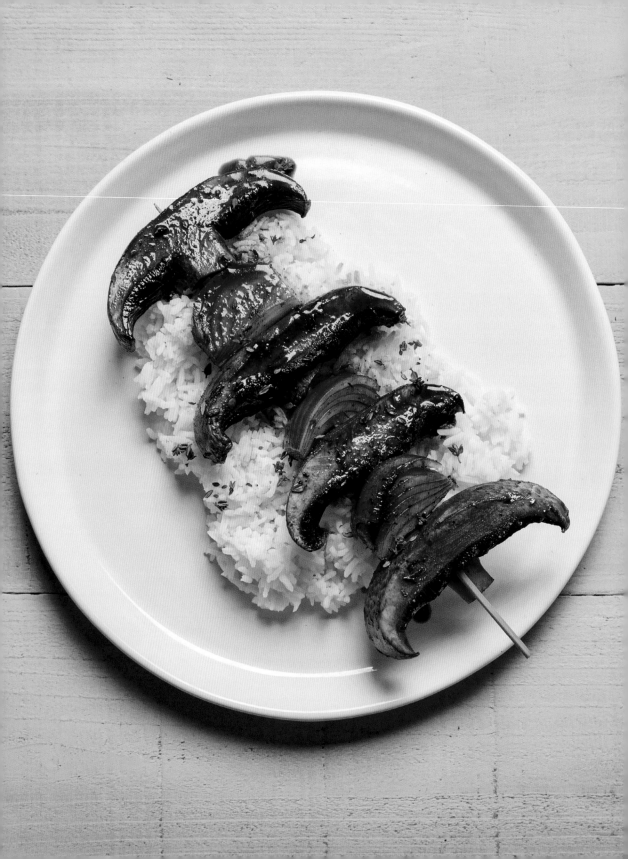

You're a Jerk! (Portland Jerk Mushrooms)

Serves 4

Drawing inspiration from the lively vibes of Portland parish, a small area in Jamaica that has a vibrant Jamaican food scene, this dish is a mingling of bold flavors, down-home mushrooms and a whisper of jerk spice that'll two-step on your taste buds. It's a culinary escapade that captures the very spirit of this area's groundbreaking gastronomy. Savor this plant-based delight and let Portland's one-of-a-kind flavors whisk you away on a ride of pure culinary joy!

2 tsp (10 ml) soy sauce

1 tbsp (15 ml) pure maple syrup

1 tbsp (15 ml) olive oil

3 cloves garlic, minced

2 tbsp (34 g) jerk seasoning

1 tsp dried thyme

1 tsp ground allspice

1 tsp smoked paprika

1 tsp cayenne pepper

1 tsp ground cinnamon

Salt and freshly ground black pepper

1 lb (455 g) organic portobello mushrooms, cleaned and sliced

1 red onion, sliced thinly

Cooked quinoa or rice, for serving

Fresh thyme, for garnish

Soak four wooden skewers for 30 minutes.

Meanwhile, in a small bowl, whisk together the soy sauce, maple syrup, olive oil, garlic, jerk seasoning, thyme, allspice, smoked paprika, cayenne and cinnamon, plus salt and black pepper to taste.

In a large ziplock bag or bowl, combine the sliced mushrooms and red onion. Pour the marinade over the mushrooms and onion, ensuring they are well coated. Seal the bag or cover the bowl and let marinate in the refrigerator for at least 30 minutes.

Preheat your grill or grill pan over medium-high heat.

Thread the marinated mushrooms and onion onto the skewers, alternating between them. Grill the skewers for 10 to 12 minutes, turning occasionally, until the mushrooms are tender and slightly charred.

Serve the jerk mushrooms over cooked quinoa or rice, garnished with fresh thyme.

Cheesy Poutine, Aye!

Serves 4

Let's take a journey up North, where the air gets colder and the folks know a thing or two about comfort food. I found myself in the heart of British Columbia, Canada, land of maple syrup and politeness, where the winters are as frosty as a Sunday morning church pew. Now, they may not know much about sweet tea, but let me tell ya, they've got a little secret called poutine that'll warm your soul like a cozy blanket on a chilly evening. I took a bite and, oh my goodness, I was in a food coma.

Potatoes

4 large russet potatoes, washed and cut into fries

2 tbsp (30 ml) olive oil

1 tsp garlic powder

1 tsp onion powder

1 tsp paprika

½ tsp salt

¼ tsp freshly ground black pepper

Vegan Cheese Sauce

1 cup (140 g) raw cashews, soaked in hot water for 1 hour, then drained

1 cup (240 ml) unflavored, unsweetened oat milk (or any plant-based milk of your choice)

¼ cup (32 g) nutritional yeast

2 tbsp (16 g) tapioca starch

1 tbsp (15 ml) fresh lemon juice

1 tsp white miso paste

½ tsp garlic powder

½ tsp onion powder

½ tsp mustard powder

Salt and freshly ground black pepper

Chopped fresh chives, for garnish

Vegan gravy (optional)

Preheat your oven to 425°F (220°C).

In a large bowl, toss the cut potatoes with olive oil, garlic powder, onion powder, paprika, salt and pepper until evenly coated. Spread them in a single layer on a baking sheet. Bake the fries for 30 to 35 minutes, or until golden brown and crispy, flipping them halfway through.

While the fries bake, prepare the cheese sauce: In a blender, combine all of the ingredients for the vegan cheese sauce. Blend until smooth.

Transfer the cheese sauce to a small saucepan and heat over low heat, stirring continuously to avoid lumps. Heat for 2 to 4 minutes or until the mixture thickens, resembling the consistency of melted cheese. If the mixture does form lumps, add 1 teaspoon of water to thin it out. Remove from the heat.

Once the fries are done, arrange them on a serving plate or dish. Pour the warm vegan cheese sauce generously over the fries.Garnish with chopped fresh chives and serve immediately. For an extra touch, you can also drizzle vegan gravy over the top, if desired.

Mushroom Babs

Serves 4

This is an incredibly delish dish I make during summer when my friends and I are sitting around the pool. "Babs" is a play on "kebabs," a street food delight that has bold flavors and is known around the world. When you bite into one of these Mushroom Babs, you'll feel like you are at a street market, surrounded by sizzling grills and the tempting allure of street vendors. These kebabs offer a symphony of flavors that resonate with well-traveled tastes. This fusion dish brings together the vibrant spirit of Greek culture. These will be your favorite, I promise.

Marinade

¼ cup (50 ml) olive oil

¼ cup (60 ml) coconut liquid aminos

1 tbsp (15 ml) agave syrup

1 tsp smoked paprika

1 tsp ground cumin

1 tsp za'atar

1 tsp garlic powder

½ tsp cayenne pepper, or to taste

Salt and freshly ground black pepper

Kebabs

1 lb (455 g) assorted mushrooms (cremini, shiitake, oyster)

1 red bell pepper, seeded and cut into chunks

1 red onion, cut into wedges

1 medium-sized zucchini, sliced

Soak four wooden skewers in water for 30 minutes.

Prepare the marinade: In a small bowl, whisk together the olive oil, coconut liquid aminos, agave, paprika, cumin, za'atar, garlic powder and cayenne, plus salt and black pepper to taste until well combined.

Prepare the mushrooms: Clean the mushrooms and cut any large ones into bite-sized pieces. Place the mushrooms, bell pepper, red onion and zucchini slices in a large bowl.

Pour the marinade over the vegetables, ensuring they are well coated. Allow them to marinate for at least 30 minutes at room temperature, or refrigerate for a few hours for enhanced flavor.

Prepare the kebabs: Preheat your grill or grill pan over medium-high heat.

Thread the marinated mushrooms, bell pepper, red onion and zucchini onto the soaked wooden skewers, alternating among the different ingredients. Grill the kebabs for 10 to 12 minutes, turning occasionally, until the vegetables are charred and cooked to your liking.

Serve the Southern-spiced vegan babs hot off the grill.

The Gyro

Serves 4

Inspired by the rich tapestry of Texan-Mediterranean fusion in the heart of southern Texas, where culinary traditions thrive like a desert bloom, this recipe pays homage to my roots. Growing up in the Lone Star State, I've embraced the spirit of adventure and decided to infuse the classic gyro with a touch of Texas charm.

Tip: Serve with a side of pickled jalapeños for an extra kick.

Gyro

2 cups (200 g) vital wheat gluten

1 cup (240 ml) vegetable stock

2 tbsp (30 ml) olive oil, divided

1 tbsp (15 ml) soy sauce

1 tsp smoked paprika

1 tsp garlic powder

1 tsp onion powder

1 tsp dried oregano

½ tsp freshly ground black pepper

Tzatziki Sauce

1 cup (230 g) dairy-free yogurt

1 cucumber, diced finely

2 cloves garlic, minced

1 tbsp (4 g) chopped fresh dill

1 tbsp (15 ml) fresh lemon juice

Salt and freshly ground black pepper

For Assembly

Pita bread (enough for serving)

Sliced tomato

Sliced red onion

Preheat your oven to 350°F (180°C).

Prepare the gyro: In a large bowl, combine the vital wheat gluten, vegetable stock, 1 tablespoon (15 ml) of the olive oil, soy sauce, smoked paprika, garlic powder, onion powder, oregano and pepper. Whisk the ingredients together well, then knead the mixture for a few minutes until it comes together.

Shape the mixture into a 3- to 4-inch (8- to 10-cm)-thick log and wrap it tightly in parchment paper, like a sausage. Bake for 45 minutes, turning the log halfway through.

While the gyro protein bakes, prepare the tzatziki sauce: In a small bowl, mix together the dairy-free yogurt, cucumber, garlic, dill and lemon juice, plus salt and pepper to taste. Refrigerate until ready to use.

Once baked, remove the gyro protein from the oven and let cool slightly. Unwrap and slice into thin strips.

Heat a medium-sized skillet over medium-high heat and add the remaining tablespoon (15 ml) of olive oil. Sear the protein strips until browned and slightly crispy on the edges.

To assemble, warm the pita bread and fill with the sliced protein, tomatoes, red onion and a generous drizzle of tzatziki sauce.

Authentic Falafel

Serves 2 or 3

Falafel has earned its rightful place as a beloved street food across the globe. Originating in the Middle East, it has transcended borders, captivating taste buds with its irresistible blend of textures and spices. Combining traditional Middle Eastern flavors, these chickpea-based delights offer a unique and satisfying experience.

2 cups (330 g) canned chickpeas, drained and rinsed

½ large onion, chopped roughly

3 cloves garlic, minced

1 cup (60 g) fresh parsley, chopped

⅓ cup (5 g) fresh cilantro, chopped

½ cup (60 g) vegan bread crumbs

2 tbsp (15 g) organic all-purpose, unenriched, unbleached flour

1½ tsp (3.5 g) ground cumin

1 tsp ground coriander

¼ tsp cayenne pepper

Salt and freshly ground black pepper

Coconut oil or avocado oil, for frying

In a food processor, combine the chickpeas, onion, garlic, parsley and cilantro. Pulse until the mixture becomes a coarse paste, then transfer the mixture to a large bowl. Add the vegan bread crumbs, flour, cumin, coriander and cayenne, plus salt and black pepper to taste. Mix well to combine.

Form the mixture into golf ball–sized rounds and flatten slightly into a patty shape.

Heat the coconut oil in a skillet over medium heat. Fry the falafel patties until golden brown on both sides, 3 to 4 minutes per side.

Remove the falafel patties from the skillet and place them on a paper towel-lined plate to absorb any excess oil.

Serve the falafel patties in pita bread or alongside your favorite hummus, and enjoy the unique fusion of flavors!

Street Empanadas

Serves 12

Embark on a street food adventure with these savory and delightful vegan empanadas. Inspired by the bustling markets and lively flavors of Latin street cuisine, this recipe captures the essence of handheld comfort. These empanadas are packed with flavor and the earthy taste of delicious mushrooms, and are perfect for any occasion!

Dough

2½ cups (313 g) organic all-purpose, unenriched, unbleached flour, plus more for dusting

½ cup (114 g) vegan butter, cold and diced

1 tsp sea salt

⅓ cup (80 ml) unflavored, unsweetened oat milk (or any plant-based milk of your choice)

Filling

2 tbsp (30 ml) olive oil

1 onion, chopped finely

3 cloves garlic, minced

3 cups (200 g) organic shiitake mushrooms

1 tsp ground cumin

1 tsp smoked paprika

½ tsp chili powder

½ cup (123 g) tomato sauce

¼ cup (27 g) dry sun-dried tomatoes, chopped

Salt and freshly ground black pepper

1 qt (946 ml) coconut oil, for frying

Prepare the dough: In a large bowl, combine the flour and cold, diced vegan butter and salt. Use your fingers to rub the butter into the flour until it resembles crumbs.

Slowly add the cold oat milk, mixing until the dough comes together. Form a ball, wrap it in plastic wrap and refrigerate for at least 30 minutes.

Prepare the filling: In a large skillet, heat the olive oil over medium heat. Sauté the onion and garlic until softened. Add your mushrooms, cumin, smoked paprika and chili powder. Cook for 5 to 7 minutes, or until the mushrooms are deeply browned and no liquid is in the pan.

Stir in the tomato sauce and sun-dried tomatoes, plus salt and pepper to taste. Simmer for an additional 5 minutes, or until the mixture thickens. Remove from the heat, let cool, then cover and refrigerate until chilled, about 1 hour.

Remove the dough and filling from the refrigerator. Roll out the chilled dough on a floured surface to ½-inch (1.3-cm) thickness and cut circles, using a 4- to 6-inch (10- to 15-cm)-diameter round cutter. Spoon a portion of the filling onto each dough circle.

Fold the dough over, forming a half-moon shape and seal the edges by pressing with a fork.

In a large, deep skillet, heat the coconut oil over medium heat to 375°F (190°C). Fry the empanadas, only two at a time, for 2 to 3 minutes on each side, or until golden brown on both sides.

Transfer to a wire rack and serve while hot.

Melon Poke Bowl

Serves 2

Embark on a culinary journey with a burst of freshness and vibrant flavors that will transport you to a tropical paradise. In this plant-powered rendition, we're elevating the succulent cubes of juicy melons with a zesty lime infusion, creating a bowl that's not only light and satisfying but also a symphony of refreshing tastes. Grab your chopsticks and let's dive into this vegan delight that's as invigorating as a sip of freshly squeezed limeade on a sunny day.

Marinade

3 tbsp (45 ml) soy sauce or tamari

1 tbsp (15 ml) rice vinegar

1 tbsp (15 ml) pure maple syrup

1 tsp sesame oil

1 tsp grated fresh ginger

1 clove garlic, minced

Melon Poke Bowl

2 cups (300 g) seeded and cubed watermelon

2 cups (320 g) seeded and cubed cantaloupe

1 cup (135 g) peeled and julienned cucumber

1 avocado, peeled, pitted and sliced

¼ cup (29 g) thinly sliced radish

1 tbsp (15 g) pickled ginger

2 tbsp (16 g) black or white sesame seeds, plus more for garnish

2 green onions, sliced thinly, plus more for garnish

Juice of 1 lime

2 cups (400 g) cooked sushi rice or (370 g) quinoa

Prepare the marinade: In a small bowl, whisk together the soy sauce, rice vinegar, maple syrup, sesame oil, ginger and garlic. Set aside.

Prepare the poke bowl: In a large bowl, combine the watermelon and cantaloupe cubes, cucumber, avocado slices, radish slices, pickled ginger, sesame seeds and green onions. Gently pour the marinade over the melon mixture and toss until everything is well coated. Allow it to marinate for at least 10 minutes for the flavors to meld.

Squeeze fresh lime juice over the marinated melon mixture, giving it a zesty kick. Toss gently to incorporate the lime infusion.

Divide the sushi rice or quinoa between two bowls. Top with the marinated melon mixture, arranging it on one side of each bowl. Sprinkle additional sesame seeds and green onions for garnish.

Bang! Bang! Chimichanga

Serves 4

As far as Tex-Mex food goes, this one is one that I can't stop making. The peppers, mushrooms and vegan Cheddar all meld together to create this hit of a dish. You can make these for lunch or dinner, or even freeze it for later in the week.

3 tbsp (45 ml) olive oil, divided
1 cup (150 g) seeded and diced bell pepper
1 cup (150 g) corn kernels
4 cups (268 g) shiitake mushrooms, sliced
1 cup (150 g) cherry tomatoes, halved
1 cup (172 g) cooked and mashed black beans
1 tsp ground cumin
1 tsp chili powder
1 tsp garlic powder
Salt and freshly ground black pepper
4 large flour tortillas
1 cup (113 g) shredded vegan Cheddar cheese
Chopped fresh cilantro, for garnish
Vegan sour cream and guacamole (for serving)

In a large skillet over medium heat, heat 1 tablespoon (15 ml) of the olive oil and sauté the bell peppers, corn and shiitake mushrooms until tender. Add the cherry tomatoes, mashed black beans, cumin, chili powder and garlic powder, plus salt and pepper to taste. Cook until well combined and heated through.

Warm the tortillas in a separate pan over low heat or in a microwave until heated through.

Spoon the spicy bean and veggie mixture onto the center of each tortilla, top with vegan Cheddar and fold into a burrito.

In the same large skillet, heat the remaining 2 tablespoons (30 ml) of the olive oil over medium heat. Place the chimichangas, seam side down, in the skillet and cook until golden brown and crispy on all sides.

Serve the chimichangas with a sprinkle of fresh cilantro and a side of vegan sour cream and guacamole. Enjoy your spicy shiitake Chimichanga fiesta!

Na-Na-Naan

Serves 8

Let's whip up a batch of the most delicious naan bread you ever did taste. This recipe is an Indian classic and let me tell you, it's going to be bread that you eat with everything. I love pairing it with Indian Samosa (page 112) or *chaat*, and using it for wraps with veggies and any vegan faux meats. Go into the kitchen and grab your apron, and let's get cookin'—we're about to make some naan magic.

1 tsp active dry yeast

1 tsp organic granulated sugar

1 tsp baking soda

½ tsp baking powder

1 tsp salt

2½ cups (313 g) organic all-purpose, unenriched, unbleached flour, plus more for dusting

3 tbsp (45 ml) olive oil

1 cup (230 g) plain vegan Greek yogurt, at room temperature

¼ cup (60 ml) melted vegan butter, plus more for brushing

2 tsp (6 g) garlic powder

2 tsp (0.6 g) dried parsley flakes

Warm vegan butter, for brushing

Place the yeast into warm water according to the package instructions.

In a large bowl, mix together the sugar, baking soda, baking powder, salt and flour. Add the olive oil, vegan Greek yogurt and melted vegan butter, then give it all a good stir until a dough forms.

Knead that dough on a floured surface until it's smooth and elastic—about 5 minutes or so.

Add the ball of dough back in the bowl, cover it with a clean cloth and let rest for about 30 minutes. Meanwhile, preheat your oven to 500°F (260°C).

Divide the rested dough into eight equal-sized pieces and roll out into 6- to 8-inch (15- to 20-cm)-long ovals. Place them on a baking sheet and sprinkle with the garlic powder and parsley.

Bake for 3 to 5 minutes, or until golden brown and irresistible. Brush the naan with warm vegan butter and serve.

Indian Samosa

Serves 4 or 5

I love samosas. Whenever I'm at an Indian restaurant, it's the first thing I order from the appetizer menu. Now, these samosas are original. I decided to combine some things that I love: sweet potatoes, black-eyed peas and smoked vegan sausages. Ohhhh baby, this one is like the South meets India. When you make these for your friends, they'll be talking about these samosas from Texas to the Mississippi Delta.

2 cups (250 g) organic all-purpose, unenriched, unbleached flour

½ cup (114 g) unsalted vegan butter, melted

½ cup (115 g) plain vegan Greek yogurt

1 tsp kosher salt

1 cup (133 g) cooked and mashed sweet potato

1 cup (165 g) cooked black-eyed peas

1 cup (170 g) diced vegan smoked sausage (I prefer Field Roast® brand Smoked Apple & Sage Sausage)

¼ cup (13 g) chopped green onions

2 tbsp (2 g) chopped fresh cilantro

1 tsp ground cumin

1 tsp curry powder

½ tsp cayenne pepper

1 qt (946 ml) coconut oil, for frying

In a large bowl, mix together the flour, melted vegan butter, vegan Greek yogurt and salt until it forms a smooth dough. Let rest for 10 minutes while we get to the good stuff.

In a medium-sized bowl, combine the sweet potato, black-eyed peas, smoked sausage, green onions, cilantro, cumin, curry powder and cayenne, and give it a good stir. Be sure your mixture has cooled before adding the mixture to the dough.

Roll out the rested dough into thin disks, preferably a scant ⅛ inch (2 mm) thick. Aim for 6 inches (15 cm) in diameter. Cut through the center to make two half-moons Pick up one half-moon, forming a cone shape by bringing the corners of the straight edge together, overlapping the straight edges slightly.

Spoon a generous dollop of the filling onto each cone and fold it up into a triangle. Dampen the edges of the open end with water to help the cone stick together. Press the edges tightly to seal, leaving a small flat border at the top.

In a large skillet, heat up that coconut oil. Once hot, fry the samosas until crispy and golden, 6 to 8 minutes.

Drain them on a metal rack and allow them to cool for a minute or two before serving.

England's Famous Fish & Chips

Serves 4

Now, I haven't crossed the pond to the U.K. but I hear that they make a mean fish. Well, in the South we can fry up anything and make it taste delicious. Before I was vegan, I was an avid fisherman and I could fry up that fish like no other. But I'm vegan now and I let the fish swim and mind their business; I can still get my "vish," but it's not from the water.

Chips

4 large russet potatoes, peeled and cut into thick strips

2 tbsp (30 ml) olive oil

1 tsp onion powder

1 tsp garlic powder

1 tsp paprika

¼ tsp cayenne pepper

Vegan Fish

2 (9-oz [260-g]) cans young green banana blossoms, drained (I suggest Nature's Charm brand)

1 cup (125 g) organic all-purpose, unenriched, unbleached flour

1 cup (140 g) cornmeal

1 cup (130 g) cornstarch

1 tsp baking powder

1 tsp garlic powder

1 tsp onion powder

1 tsp smoked paprika

½ tsp ground turmeric

1 tsp salt-free Creole seasoning (I use Tony Chachere's® No Salt Creole Seasoning)

Salt and freshly ground black pepper

1½ cups (355 ml) cold sparkling water

1 qt (946 ml) avocado oil, for frying

Prepare the chips: Preheat your over to 450°F (230°C).

In a medium-sized bowl, toss your potato strips with the olive oil, then add the onion powder, garlic powder, paprika and cayenne, and toss again. Spread the strips on a baking sheet and bake for 30 minutes, or until golden brown and crispy, flipping the potatoes halfway through.

Prepare the vegan fish: Open up the banana blossoms and trim away any tough outer leaves. Cut the blossoms into pieces resembling fish filets.

In a bowl, combine the flour, cornmeal, cornstarch, baking powder, garlic powder, onion powder, smoked paprika, turmeric and Creole seasoning, plus salt and pepper to taste. Pour in the cold sparkling water and whisk until you have a smooth, thick batter.

In a large, deep skillet, heat the avocado oil to about 350°F (180°C).

Dip each piece of banana blossom into the batter, ensuring it's well coated, and gently place it in the hot oil. Fry, turning occasionally, until golden brown and crispy, 6 to 8 minutes.

Use a slotted spoon to transfer the vegan fish to a paper towel-lined plate, to absorb any excess oil. Serve your crispy banana blossom fish with Tantalizing Tartar Sauce (page 149).

Spicy Spring Rolls

Serves 12

Okay, I could eat spring rolls every day. These are my favorite street food and this recipe will take your taste buds on a journey. They are packed with plant-based goodness and will make your kitchen feel like a global food market. Whether you're a seasoned plant-based eater or just diving into the world of vegan delights, these rolls are your ticket to a street food adventure.

Spring Rolls

1 cup (140 g) cooked vermicelli noodles, cooled

1 cup (90 g) shredded purple cabbage

1 cup (130 g) matchstick-cut carrots

1 cup (130 g) julienned cucumber

1 cup (70 g) thinly sliced organic baby bella mushrooms

½ cup (8 g) fresh cilantro leaves

½ cup (20 g) fresh mint leaves

¼ cup (35 g) chopped peanuts

12 rice paper wrappers

Spicy Peanut Sauce

¼ cup (64 g) peanut butter

2 tbsp (30 ml) soy sauce

1 tbsp (15 ml) Sriracha

1 tbsp (15 ml) rice vinegar

1 tbsp (15 ml) pure maple syrup

1 tsp sesame oil

1 clove garlic, minced

Water to thin, if needed

Prepare the spring rolls: In a large bowl, combine the vermicelli noodles, purple cabbage, carrots, cucumber, mushrooms, cilantro, mint and peanuts. Toss gently to mix everything together.

Fill a shallow dish with warm water. Dip a rice paper wrapper into the water for about 5 seconds, just until it softens. Lay it flat on a clean surface.

Place a generous amount of the filling in the center of the rice paper wrapper. Fold the sides of the wrapper over the filling, then fold the bottom and roll tightly. Repeat for the remaining wrappers and filling.

Prepare the peanut sauce: In a small bowl, whisk together the peanut butter, soy sauce, Sriracha, rice vinegar, maple syrup, sesame oil and garlic. If the sauce is too thick, add water gradually until you reach your desired consistency.

Arrange the spring rolls on a serving platter and serve with the spicy peanut sauce, for dipping.

SWEET THANGS

Indulge your sweet tooth with this section of the cookbook. Your mouth will water as you craft these irresistible recipes. Y'all already know that sweets make up half of the good stuff at street stalls and festivals! Let's get into some of my favorites.

Sweet American Donut

Serves 12

Bless the whisk and sprinkle it with flour, because I love the sweet world of vegan donuts. You are in for a treat with these pillowy delights that are bursting with cinnamon, nutmeg and all the good you can imagine. A touch of oat milk keeps things plant-based and downright delicious. You'll be eating these weekly for breakfast with your coffee or tea.

Donuts

All-purpose baking spray, for pan

2 cups (250 g) organic all-purpose, unenriched, unbleached flour

1 cup (200 g) organic granulated sugar

2 tsp (9 g) baking powder

½ tsp baking soda

½ tsp salt

1 tsp ground cinnamon

½ tsp ground nutmeg

1 cup (240 ml) unflavored, unsweetened oat milk (or any plant-based milk of your choice)

¼ cup (60 ml) coconut oil

1 tsp vanilla extract

1 tbsp (15 ml) apple cider vinegar

Cinnamon Sugar Coating

¼ cup (60 ml) melted vegan butter

½ cup (100 g) organic granulated sugar

1 tsp ground cinnamon

Prepare the donuts: Preheat your oven to 375°F (190°C) and spray a 12-well donut pan with all-purpose baking spray.

In a large bowl, whisk together the flour, sugar, baking powder, baking soda, salt, cinnamon and nutmeg.

In a small bowl, mix together the oat milk, coconut oil, vanilla and vinegar. Add the oat milk mixture to the flour mixture and stir until just combined.

Fill each donut well about two-thirds full of the batter. Smooth the tops with a spatula.

Bake for 12 to 15 minutes, or until a toothpick inserted into a donut comes out clean. Remove from the oven and let cool slightly.

While the donuts bake, prepare the cinnamon sugar coating: Pour the melted vegan butter into a small bowl. In a separate small bowl, mix together the sugar and cinnamon.

As soon as the donuts are cool enough to handle, dip each one into the melted vegan butter, then roll it in the cinnamon-sugar mixture until fully coated. Place the coated donuts on a wire rack to cool completely.

Not Buc-ee's Candied Pecans

Serves 8

Everything is bigger in Texas, and when I visited Buc-ee's, I was in awe. Not by the size of the popular convenience store, but the smell of the candied nuts. The ladies behind the station worked their magic to make sure each nut was sugar-coated, crispy and delicious to the last bite. You don't have to go to Buc-ee's anymore . . . You can make these pecans in your house. And it's not PUH-CAN, it's PEE-CAN, down here in East Texas.

4 cups (400 g) pecan halves

½ cup (120 ml) pure maple syrup

¼ cup (60 g) packed organic brown sugar

¼ cup (60 ml) unflavored, unsweetened oat milk (or any plant-based milk of your choice)

1 tsp ground cinnamon

½ tsp ground nutmeg

½ tsp salt

1 tsp vanilla extract

Preheat your oven to 325°F (160°C) and line a baking sheet with parchment paper.

In a large bowl, combine the pecan halves, maple syrup, brown sugar, oat milk, cinnamon, nutmeg, salt and vanilla. Toss until the pecans are evenly coated.

Spread the pecans in a single layer on the prepared baking sheet.

Bake for 30 to 35 minutes, stirring every 10 minutes, until the pecans are caramelized and golden brown.

Remove from the oven and let them cool completely on the baking sheet. They'll continue to crisp up as they cool.

Once cooled, break apart any clusters and store the candied pecans in an airtight container.

N'awlins Beignets

Serves 12 to 15

New Orleans has irresistible beignets—a culinary ode to the city's vibrant spirit. These golden pillows of fried perfection, generously dusted with powdered sugar, are a sweet treat that captures the essence of the Big Easy. Why not bring the Big Easy into your kitchen? Get ready to savor the magic of New Orleans in each bite.

1 cup (240 ml) unflavored, unsweetened oat milk (or any plant-based milk of your choice), warmed to about 110°F (43°C)

2¼ tsp (9 g) active dry yeast

¼ cup (50 g) organic granulated sugar

3½ cups (438 g) organic all-purpose, unenriched, unbleached flour, plus more for dusting

½ tsp salt

½ tsp ground cardamom

¼ cup (57 g) vegan butter, melted

1 tsp vanilla extract

Coconut oil, for bowl

1 qt (946 ml) avocado oil, for frying

Organic powdered sugar, for dusting

In a small bowl, combine the warm oat milk, yeast and granulated sugar. Allow it to sit for 5 to 10 minutes, or until it becomes frothy.

Meanwhile, in a large bowl, whisk together the flour, salt and cardamom.

Make a well in the center of the flour mixture and pour in the yeast mixture, melted vegan butter and vanilla. Mix until a soft dough forms.

Knead the dough on a floured surface until smooth. Oil a bowl with coconut oil. Place the dough in the prepared bowl, cover with a clean kitchen towel and let rise in a warm place for 1 to 2 hours, or until doubled in size.

Once the dough has risen, roll it out on a floured surface to about ¼-inch (6-mm) thickness. Cut the dough into squares or rectangles. In a large, deep skillet or fryer, heat avocado oil to 350°F (180°C).

Working in batches, carefully drop the cut dough pieces into the hot avocado oil, frying each side until golden brown, usually 2 to 3 minutes per side.

Use a slotted spoon to transfer the golden beignets to a paper towel–lined plate, to absorb any excess oil. Then, place them on a wire rack to prevent them from sweating. Dust the warm beignets generously with powdered sugar and serve while hot.

El Churro

Serves 20

Hey there, sweet souls! Brace yourselves for a plant-powered journey into the world of heavenly churros that's sure to leave your taste buds doing the cha-cha. These aren't your average churros—they're a crispy delight, generously dusted with cinnamon sugar. So, grab your apron and let's cook up a batch of these vegan churros!

1 cup (240 ml) water
½ cup (114 g) vegan butter
¼ tsp sea salt
1 cup (125 g) organic all-purpose, unenriched, unbleached flour
3 tbsp (45 ml) aquafaba (liquid from canned chickpeas)
1 tsp vanilla extract
1 qt (946 ml) coconut oil, for frying
½ cup (100 g) organic granulated sugar
1 tbsp (7 g) ground cinnamon

In a medium-sized saucepan over medium heat, bring the water, vegan butter and salt to a boil.

Lower the heat to low and stir in the flour until the mixture forms a smooth dough. Remove from the heat and let cool for a couple of minutes.

Beat in the aquafaba, 1 tablespoon (15 ml) at a time, ensuring it's fully incorporated. Stir in the vanilla.

In a large, deep skillet, heat the coconut oil over medium heat until it reaches 375°F (190°C).

Spoon the vegan churro dough into a piping bag fitted with a star tip. Carefully pipe 5-inch (12.5-cm)-long strips of dough directly into the hot oil. Fry until golden brown, 2 to 3 minutes per side.

Use a slotted spoon to transfer the golden vegan churros to a paper towel–lined plate, to absorb any excess oil.

In a shallow bowl, combine the sugar and cinnamon. Roll the warm churros in the mixture until generously coated.

Serve these delightful vegan churros warm and savor the crunchy, cinnamon-kissed goodness!

Strawberry Nice Cream

Serves 6

Nice cream is as sweet as a southern sunset and smoother than a front porch swing. With a hint of cardamom and creamy oat milk, you won't miss regular ice cream. I make this in the summer when the weather is hot and I need something to cool me off. My nice cream gets the job done.

4 cups (596 g) frozen strawberries

½ cup (120 ml) pure maple syrup

1 tsp ground cardamom

1½ cups (355 ml) unflavored, unsweetened oat milk (or any plant-based milk of your choice)

1 tsp vanilla extract

In a blender, combine the frozen strawberries, maple syrup, cardamom, oat milk and vanilla. Blend until silky smooth.

Pour the mixture into a loaf pan or any container with a lid. Freeze for at least 4 hours, or until firm.

When it's time to serve, scoop the nice cream into a bowl or cone. Top it off with your favorite vegan sprinkles or sliced fresh strawberries if you're looking to fancy it up.

Lucile's Vegan Pound Cake

Serves 12

My Aunt Cile makes the best pound cakes and I had to make one that you can enjoy anytime of the year. Now, this pound cake recipe is one that will make you slap somebody because it's so good. Now, it's a tie between my Aunt Cile and my grandma Bennie on who can make the best pound cakes. This one will be a treat for any occasion!

Pound Cake

2 cups (454 g) vegan butter, at room temperature

3 cups (600 g) organic granulated sugar

1½ cups (355 ml) vegan egg substitute (I prefer JUST Egg brand)

3¼ cups (406 g) organic all-purpose, unenriched, unbleached flour, plus more for dusting

1 tsp vanilla extract

1 tsp lemon extract

½ cup (120 ml) unflavored, unsweetened oat milk (or any plant-based milk of your choice), at room temperature

1 tsp coconut oil

Icing

3 cups (360 g) organic powdered sugar

1 tsp vanilla extract

⅓ cup (80 ml) oat milk (or any plant-based milk of your choice)

Prepare the pound cake: Preheat your oven to 350°F (180°C).

In a large bowl, combine the vegan butter and granulated sugar, and mix until light and fluffy with an electric mixer. Gradually add the vegan egg, beating well after each addition.

Next, add the organic flour and mix well until the batter becomes creamy. Slowly incorporate the vanilla and lemon extracts while mixing, as well as the oat milk. Mix until just combined; avoid overmixing.

Oil a 10-inch (25-cm) Bundt pan with the coconut oil and be sure to use a pinch or two of flour to coat your pan; remove any excess flour by dumping it onto a plate. You want your Bundt pan to be lightly floured to prevent the cake from sticking to the pan. Pour the batter into the prepared pan, spreading it out evenly.

Bake for 1 hour, or until a toothpick inserted into the center comes out clean.

Remove from the oven and allow the pound cake to cool in the pan for about 15 minutes before transferring it to a wire rack to cool completely.

Prepare the icing: In a small bowl, whisk together the powdered sugar, vanilla and oat milk until you achieve a smooth, pourable consistency. Once the pound cake is completely cooled, drizzle the glaze over the top, letting it cascade down the sides. Allow the glaze to set for a bit before slicing into this delectable pound cake.

Bananacue

Serves 6

In the Filipino culture, *banacue* is tantalizing. The aroma of caramelized bananas mingles with the sizzle of an open flame. I love everything about bananas. This classic treat combines the sweetness of ripe bananas, draped in a luscious blend of brown sugar, vanilla and a hint of cinnamon. This creation is a nod to warm memories, evoking the joy of chill afternoons on the porch around a grill. These will be a hit when your friends come over to gather. They'll be amazed at how good bananas are on a grill.

6 ripe yet firm bananas

1 cup (225 g) organic brown sugar

½ cup (120 ml) water

1 tsp vanilla extract

¼ tsp ground cinnamon

Soak six wooden skewers in water for 30 minutes.

Meanwhile, peel the bananas and cut them into halves or thirds, depending on your preferred size. Thread each banana onto a soaked wooden skewer, making sure it's secure but not too tight.

In a medium-sized saucepan over medium heat, combine the brown sugar, water, vanilla and cinnamon. Stir until the sugar is completely dissolved and the mixture forms a syrup. Allow it to simmer for a few minutes until it slightly thickens.

Lower the heat to low and carefully dip each banana skewer into the syrup, ensuring it's well coated. Place the coated bananas on a parchment paper–lined tray or plate, allowing the syrup to cool and harden slightly.

Heat a grill pan or nonstick skillet over medium heat. Grill each banana skewer for 2 to 3 minutes on each side, or until they develop a golden-brown caramelized coating.

Once grilled to perfection, remove the bananacue from the heat and let them cool for a few minutes before serving.

Big Texas State Fair Funnel Cake

Serves 4

The State Fair of Texas is known throughout Texas for food, good times and great fun. I had my first funnel cake experience at this fair and I can still remember it like it was yesterday. Now, I wasn't vegan then, so I had to work something up for you to enjoy. This will take you back to your childhood days of your local county fair. Make this in the fall or winter when the weather is cool outside.

2 cups (250 g) organic all-purpose, unenriched, unbleached flour

2 tbsp (16 g) cornstarch

¼ cup (50 g) organic granulated sugar

1 tsp baking powder

½ tsp baking soda

¼ tsp salt

1½ cups (355 ml) unflavored, unsweetened oat milk (or any plant-based milk of your choice)

1 tbsp (15 ml) apple cider vinegar

1 tsp vanilla extract

1 qt (946 ml) coconut oil, for frying

Organic powdered sugar, for dusting

In a large bowl, whisk together the flour, cornstarch, granulated sugar, baking powder, baking soda and salt.

In a small bowl, combine the oat milk, vinegar and vanilla. Let sit for a few minutes to curdle slightly.

Pour the oat milk mixture into the flour mixture, whisking until you have a smooth batter. The consistency should be like pancake batter.

In a large, deep skillet, heat the coconut oil over medium-high heat. The oil is ready when a small drop of batter sizzles and floats to the top.

Using a funnel or squeeze bottle, pour the batter into the hot oil, moving in a circular motion to create a lacy pattern. Fry for 2 to 3 minutes on each side, or until golden brown. Carefully remove the funnel cake from the oil using tongs and place it on a paper towel–lined plate to absorb any excess oil.

Dust the funnel cake generously with powdered sugar and serve warm.

A Food Truck in Austin's Mango Sticky Rice

Serves 4

I was visiting Austin a few summers ago with my friend and he introduced me to a food truck that served mango sticky rice. Now, I've never had this dish before and when I tried it, a foodgasm occurred. I was in love! This tropical delight brings together the sweetness of ripe mangoes and the comforting creaminess of coconut-infused sticky rice. It's like a little taste of paradise in every bite.

1 cup (200 g) uncooked glutinous rice

1½ cups (355 ml) canned coconut milk

½ cup (100 g) organic granulated sugar

¼ tsp salt

2 ripe mangoes, peeled, pitted and sliced

1 tbsp (8 g) black sesame seeds, for garnish

Fresh mint leaves, for garnish

Rinse the glutinous rice under cold water until the water runs clear. Soak the rice in water for at least 30 minutes or up to overnight.

Drain the soaked rice and steam it in a bamboo or metal steamer for 25 to 30 minutes, or until the grains become translucent and sticky.

While the rice steams, prepare a coconut sauce: In a medium-sized saucepan, combine the coconut milk, sugar and salt. Heat over medium heat until the sugar dissolves but avoid bringing it to a boil. Remove from the heat and set aside to cool.

Once the rice is done, transfer it to a large bowl. Gradually pour half of the coconut sauce over the rice, stirring gently to coat each grain. Let sit for a few minutes to absorb the flavors.

To serve, place a generous portion of the coconut-infused sticky rice on a plate. Arrange sliced mangoes on top and drizzle with the remaining coconut sauce.

Garnish the dish with black sesame seeds and fresh mint leaves for a pop of color and extra flavor.

Mrs. Bennie's German Chocolate Cupcakes

Serves 12

My grandmother "Mu," a.k.a. Mrs. Bennie, can throw down on some German chocolate cakes! Now, she hasn't been to Germany, but let me tell you, these are a hit here in East Texas. Her cakes are moist, full of flavor and rich. You can't just eat one of these cupcakes, you may eat them all. Save some for you family and friends and try not to eat them all.

Cupcakes

1½ cups (188 g) organic all-purpose, unenriched, unbleached flour

1 cup (200 g) organic granulated sugar

⅓ cup (27 g) unsweetened cocoa powder

1 tsp baking soda

½ tsp baking powder

¼ tsp salt

1 cup (240 ml) strong brewed coffee, cooled

½ cup (120 ml) melted coconut oil

2 tsp (10 ml) vanilla extract

1 tbsp (15 ml) apple cider vinegar

Coconut-Pecan Frosting

1 cup (240 ml) unflavored, unsweetened, full-fat oat milk

1 cup (225 g) packed organic brown sugar

½ cup (114 g) vegan butter

1 tsp almond extract

2 cups (160 g) shredded unsweetened coconut

1½ cups (165 g) chopped pecans

Prepare the cupcakes: Preheat your oven to 375°F (190°C) and line a 12-well muffin tin with cupcake liners.

In a large bowl, whisk together the flour, granulated sugar, cocoa powder, baking soda, baking powder and salt.

In a small bowl, combine the brewed coffee, melted coconut oil, vanilla and vinegar. Pour the coffee mixture into the flour mixture and stir until just combined. Avoid overmixing.

Divide the batter equally among the cupcake liners, filling each about two-thirds full. Bake for 25 to 35 minutes, or until a tooth-pick inserted into the center of a cupcake comes out clean.

While the cupcakes cool, prepare the frosting: In a medium-sized saucepan over medium heat, combine the oat milk, brown sugar, vegan butter and almond extract. Stir until the sugar is dissolved and the mixture is smooth.

Add the shredded coconut and chopped pecans, stirring continuously until the frosting thickens. Remove from heat and let cool.

Once the cupcakes are completely cool, generously frost each one with the luscious coconut-pecan mixture.

Big Momma's Teacakes

Everyone is my family knew my Big Momma (great-grandmother) made the best teacakes. Folks would say, "Now, Momma put her foot in them teacakes!" That meant they were good. She always had them placed on her kitchen table for all the family to come by and get them a couple. They were crispy on the outside and warm and soft in the inside. Now, I get to share her teacakes with you.

1 cup (227 g) vegan butter, at room temperature

1½ cups (300 g) organic granulated sugar

2 tbsp (30 ml) unflavored, unsweetened oat milk (or any plant-based milk of your choice)

½ cup (125 g) unsweetened applesauce

1 tsp vanilla extract

3 cups (375 g) organic all-purpose, unenriched, unbleached flour, plus more for dusting

½ tsp baking soda

½ tsp baking powder

¼ tsp salt

Preheat your oven to 350°F (180°C) and line a baking sheet with parchment paper. In a large bowl, cream together the vegan butter and sugar until light and fluffy.

Add the oat milk, applesauce and vanilla to the sugar mixture. Mix well. In a medium-sized bowl, whisk together the flour, baking soda, baking powder and salt.

Gradually add the flour mixture to the sugar mixture, mixing until a soft dough forms. Roll the dough into a ball and refrigerate for at least 30 minutes.

Once chilled, roll out the dough on a floured surface to about ¼-inch (6-mm) thickness. Use cookie cutters to cut out round shapes and place them on the prepared baking sheet.

Bake for 10 to 12 minutes, or until the edges are lightly golden.

Remove from the oven and allow the teacakes to cool on the baking sheet for a few minutes before transferring them to a wire rack to cool completely.

KEEP IT SAUCY

We're spicin' things up with a saucy twist that you can use for dipping sauces or to slather on your burger. The possibilities are endless! From Vegan Mayo (page 144) to my Texas Kickback Sauce (page 147), you'll find a sauce that you love here.

Vegan Mayo

Serves 1 or 2

Think about it. We put mayonnaise on so many things. When I was young my momma "Shirley" would slap it on all of our sammiches. She knew how to make me happy! I loved when she put it on her gourmet burgers and how it dripped off the side of the buns. Talmbout good! But the healthiest version of mayonnaise is the one that you can make in your own kitchen. And this one is 100 percent vegan and gluten-free, and contains no nuts.

½ cup (120 ml) unflavored, unsweetened oat milk (or any other plant-based milk of your choice)

1 tbsp (15 ml) apple cider vinegar

1 tsp Dijon or yellow mustard

1 tsp agave syrup

¼ tsp sea salt

½ tsp garlic powder

¼ tsp onion powder

½ cup (120 ml) olive oil

In a high-speed blender or food processor, combine the oat milk, vinegar, Dijon mustard, agave, salt, garlic powder and onion powder.

Start the blender on low speed for a few seconds to mix the ingredients.

While the blender is on low speed, slowly drizzle in the olive oil through the center opening of the lid. Continue to blend until the mayonnaise starts to thicken and emulsify. The mixture will begin to look like a traditional mayonnaise.

Taste and adjust the mayonnaise to your preference. Transfer to a small to medium-sized Mason jar or airtight container and refrigerate for 1 to 2 weeks.

Easy Ketchup

Makes 4 to 5 cups
(946 ml to 1 L)

You put your hand upon my hip, when you dip, I dip, we dip. That's one of my favorite old-school songs from the '90s and I always think about dipping some fries or something crispy into some ketchup when I hear the song. This ketchup has a bit of spice to it, but it isn't too spicy and it will be the perfect condiment that you need.

2 (28-oz [800-g]) cans crushed tomatoes
½ cup (120 ml) apple cider vinegar
¼ cup (60 ml) agave syrup
2 tsp (5 g) onion powder
2 tsp (6 g) garlic powder
1 tsp smoked paprika
½ tsp mustard powder
½ tsp ground cloves
¼ tsp cayenne pepper
Salt and freshly ground black pepper

In a large saucepan, combine the crushed tomatoes, vinegar and agave.

Place the saucepan over medium heat and bring the mixture to a gentle simmer.

Stir in the onion powder, garlic powder, smoked paprika, mustard powder, cloves and cayenne.

Let the mixture simmer for 30 to 40 minutes, stirring occasionally, until it thickens to your desired consistency.

Season the ketchup with salt and pepper to taste. Keep in mind that the flavors will intensify as it cools.

Remove the saucepan from the heat and let the ketchup cool to room temperature.

Using a blender or immersion blender, blend the ketchup until smooth. Transfer to sterilized jars or bottles and store it in the refrigerator. The ketchup will keep for 2 to 3 weeks in the fridge.

Hot Beer Cheese

Serves 2

This delicious and dairy-free alternative to traditional beer cheese will have you wanting more! And with this easy recipe, you can make it anytime. Made with plant-based ingredients, including cashews and nutritional yeast, it has a creamy flavor that pairs well with my Great American Pretzel (page 31). It can be used as a dip for chips or crackers, or as a spread on sandwiches and burgers. With its rich and satisfying taste, vegan beer cheese is a great option for vegans and nonvegans alike.

1⅓ cups (187 g) whole roasted and salted cashews

1½ cups (355 ml) unflavored, unsweetened oat milk (or any other plant-based milk of your choice), hot (180 to 200°F [82 to 95°C], just not boiling)

¼ cup (60 ml) fresh lemon juice

½ cup (90 g) pimientos, drained

1⅓ cups (171 g) nutritional yeast flakes

1 jalapeño, sliced

1 tsp kosher salt

½ tsp paprika

¼ tsp freshly ground black pepper

½ cup (120 ml) lager beer, at room temperature

In a blender, combine the cashews, oat milk, lemon juice, pimientos, nutritional yeast, jalapeño, salt, paprika, black pepper and beer. Start the blender on the lowest speed and slowly increase to its highest speed. Blend for 3 minutes, or until the cheese is creamy. Serve with my Great American Pretzel on page 31 while hot, or enjoy as fun dipper for veggies.

Texas Kickback Sauce

Makes ½ cup (120 ml)

A unique sauce that'll have you kickin' back and savorin' every bite. This zesty concoction blends the smokiness of Tabasco®, the sweetness of agave and a hit of Dijon mustard to create a sauce that's as versatile as it is flavorful.

2 tbsp (28 g) Vegan Mayo (page 144)
1 tsp minced fresh garlic
1 tsp Dijon mustard
1 tsp ketchup
½ tsp Tabasco sauce
1 tsp agave syrup

In a small bowl, combine the vegan mayonnaise, minced garlic, Dijon mustard, ketchup, Tabasco sauce and agave.

Whisk the ingredients together until well mixed, ensuring that the sauce is smooth and uniform.

Taste the sauce and adjust the seasonings according to your preference. Add more Tabasco for extra kick or agave for sweetness.

Once you achieve your desired flavor, cover the bowl and let the sauce chill in the refrigerator for at least 30 minutes, to allow the flavors to mingle.

Serve this versatile sauce alongside your favorite dishes—it's perfect for dipping, drizzling or slathering on grilled delights! This sauce will keep in the fridge for up to 2 weeks.

Ol' School Ranch

Makes 1½ cups (355 ml)

This creamy goodness with fresh herb and tang will tickle your taste buds. Whether you're fixin' up a salad or dippin' into your favorite veggie snacks, this vegan ranch is perfect for almost everything.

1 cup (225 g) Vegan Mayo (page 144)

½ cup (120 ml) plain unsweetened almond milk

1 tbsp (15 ml) apple cider vinegar

1 tbsp (4 g) chopped fresh dill

1 tbsp (3 g) chopped fresh chives

1 tsp onion powder

1 tsp garlic powder

½ tsp dried parsley

Salt and freshly ground black pepper

Squeeze of lemon juice, for extra zing (optional)

In a medium-sized bowl, whisk together the vegan mayonnaise, almond milk and vinegar until well combined.

Add the dill, chives, onion powder, garlic powder and parsley, plus salt and pepper to taste.

Continue to whisk until the herbs and spices are evenly distributed throughout the dressing. Taste the vegan ranch and adjust the seasonings according to your preference. If you like it tangy, add a squeeze of fresh lemon juice.

Cover the bowl and refrigerate for at least 30 minutes before serving, to let the flavors meld. Give the dressing a final stir before drizzling it over salads, using it as a dip or dressing up your favorite plant-based dishes. The sauce will keep in your fridge for up to 2 weeks.

Tantalizing Tartar Sauce

Makes 1½ cups (355 ml)

This delightful fusion of creamy textures, a touch of dill and a zest of lemon is set to elevate your taste experience. Whether you're indulging in a plant-based take on seafood or complementing your favorite fried green tomatoes, this tartar sauce is the secret ingredient that transforms any dish into a Southern-inspired culinary affair.

1 cup (225 g) Vegan Mayo (page 144)

2 tbsp (30 g) sweet pickle relish

1 tbsp (16 g) capers, chopped

1 tbsp (4 g) fresh dill, chopped

1 tbsp (15 g) Dijon mustard

1 tsp lemon zest

1 tsp fresh lemon juice

½ tsp onion powder

½ tsp garlic powder

Salt and freshly ground black pepper

In a mixing bowl, combine the vegan mayonnaise, sweet pickle relish, capers, dill, Dijon mustard, lemon zest and juice, onion powder and garlic powder.

Stir until well combined, ensuring an even distribution of flavors.

Taste the tartar sauce and season with salt and pepper to taste. Cover the bowl and refrigerate the vegan tartar sauce for at least 30 minutes, to allow the flavors to meld.

Once chilled, give it a final stir and serve alongside your favorite plant-based seafood. The sauce will keep in your fridge for 1 week.

Vegan Rotel

Serves 6

Back in the day, my mama, Shirley, would whip up her classic rotel that had a Southern symphony of flavors, bringing warmth to our hearts and spice to our souls. Now, I've taken a trip down memory lane, dusted off her ol' recipe and gave it a plant-based twist, so we can still savor that nostalgic goodness without leavin' behind our vegan roots. It's a taste of home, a dollop of love and a nod to the past, y'all—welcome to the veganized rotel reunion.

2 cups (475 ml) Vegan Cheese Sauce (page 96)

¼ cup (60 ml) unflavored, unsweetened oat milk

1 (10-oz [280-g]) can diced tomatoes with green chiles, drained

½ cup (64 g) nutritional yeast

¼ cup (34 g) chopped pickled jalapeños

2 tbsp (32 g) tomato paste

1 tsp onion powder

1 tsp garlic powder

½ tsp smoked paprika

Salt and freshly ground black pepper

1 (12-oz [340-g]) package vegan sausage crumbles, cooked according to package instructions

---

In a medium-sized saucepan over medium heat, combine the vegan cheese sauce, oat milk, drained diced tomatoes with green chiles, nutritional yeast, pickled jalapeños, tomato paste, onion powder, garlic powder and smoked paprika, plus salt and black pepper to taste.

Stir until well mixed and heated through, lowering the heat to low to prevent the cheese sauce from lumping. Once smooth and flavorful, remove from heat.

In a medium-sized skillet, cook the vegan sausage crumbles according to the package instructions, until browned and fully cooked.

Gently fold the cooked vegan sausage crumbles into the cheese mixture until evenly distributed. Adjust the seasoning to your liking, adding more salt, pepper or smoked paprika if desired. This sauce keeps well in the fridge for up to 2 weeks.

Garlic Cilantro Lime Sauce

Serves 4

Bursting with vibrant flavors, this unique sauce is a zesty fusion of fresh cilantro, parsley, toasted cashews and the zing of lime. As you blend these wholesome ingredients together, the kitchen will be filled with the aromatic dance of garlic and the subtle kick of red pepper flakes. Slowly streaming in extra-virgin olive oil transforms this medley into a smooth, irresistible sauce.

2 cups (32 g) fresh cilantro leaves

1 cup (60 g) fresh parsley leaves

½ cup (70 g) raw cashews, toasted

4 cloves garlic

Zest of 2 limes

Juice of 2 limes

½ cup (64 g) nutritional yeast

½ tsp red pepper flakes, or to taste

½ cup (120 ml) extra virgin olive oil

Salt and freshly ground black pepper

In a food processor, combine the cilantro, parsley, toasted cashews, garlic, lime zest and juice, nutritional yeast and red pepper flakes.

Pulse the ingredients until coarsely chopped. With the food processor running, slowly add the olive oil through the opening in the lid until the mixture forms a smooth paste.

Stop the processor and scrape down the sides, then pulse again to ensure all the ingredients are well incorporated. Taste the sauce and adjust the seasoning with salt and pepper.

Transfer the sauce to a jar or airtight container and refrigerate for at least 30 minutes, to allow the flavors to meld.

Serve this unique sauce over pasta, spread on sandwiches or use it as a flavorful marinade for grilled vegetables. This sauce keeps well for 3 to 5 days in the refrigerator.

Acknowledgments

In this cookbook, there are countless hands that have stirred, seasoned and added their unique flavors to the mix. My eternal gratitude goes to my partner in both love and creativity, Austyn Rich. Your unwavering support, late-night brainstorming sessions and unrelenting focus have made this culinary journey not only possible but infinitely more enjoyable. You're my anchor, my cheerleader and my confidant, and I can't express enough how much I love you.

To my family, the backbone of my inspiration—Mom (Shirley Edmond), Dad (Willie Edmond Sr.), Sister (Courtnee Edmond), Aunt (Lucile Peoples), Grandmother (Bennie Louise Mitchell) and my nephew (Christian Earl Williams)—your unwavering love and encouragement are the secret ingredients in every dish. You are the light that fuels my passion and I'm grateful for each of you.

A heartfelt thank-you to the incredible team at Page Street Publishing for not just believing in my culinary vision but elevating it. Special nods to Franny Donington and Meg Baskis—your support has seasoned this endeavor with a sprinkle of magic.

To the Well Agency, my ever-dedicated manager Katherine Meinhardt: Your tireless efforts go beyond the call of duty and I'm deeply appreciative.

A shout-out to the maestro of the lens, David Singeorzan, for capturing my essence with every click. You're not just a photographer; you're the visual architect of this culinary adventure. You're a beast and I'm endlessly grateful for your artistry.

In this culinary journey, your collective contributions have transformed this cookbook from a mere collection of recipes to a tapestry of love, support and creativity. Thank you all from the bottom of my heart; this cookbook reflects our shared passion and commitment to the art of good food.

About the Author

Embarking on this culinary journey takes me back to my roots, nestled in the quaint Piney Woods of East Texas, where Douglassville, a town of just 229 souls, shaped my love for good food. From the tender age of five, I made my first mark in the kitchen by crafting a pie for my grandmother, a moment etched in our shared memories. Growing up amid the culinary prowess of my grandmother and great-grandmother, I absorbed the artistry of Southern cooking—palm hot water cornbread, teacakes and biscuits that transcended mere sustenance.

Cooking isn't just a skill; it's ingrained in my heart, a passion I inherited from the resilient kitchens of East Texas. My journey to this point has been a diverse tapestry. I've worn many hats, from delving into music production, hosting events and assisting startups in the corporate arena. However, it's in the world of plant-based cuisine that I found my true calling.

In 2020, as the world braced itself, I fully immersed myself in the food realm, a decision catalyzed by a deep-seated desire to show that a vibrant, plant-based life is not only possible but delightful. Going vegan in 2017 laid the foundation, but it was a viral TikTok video, later featured on Buzzfeed, that propelled me into the spotlight. Overnight, my follower count skyrocketed and my partner, Austyn, and I found ourselves fully dedicated to building a thriving community around our shared love for food.

Beyond the virtual realm, our journey extends to the creation of "Glamping Remote" in Douglassville, Texas. Here, we aspire to meld the joy of cooking with the tranquility of nature, allowing guests to savor fresh, organic vegetables around an open fire. Today, my life revolves around crafting tantalizing recipes, producing engaging videos, capturing the essence of dishes through photography and exploring the world for culinary inspiration.

Index